Exploring the Lives of Victorian Prostitutes

Exploring the Lives of Victorian Prostitutes

Claire Richardson

PEN & SWORD
HISTORY

First published in Great Britain in 2024 by
Pen & Sword History
An imprint of Pen & Sword Books Limited
Yorkshire – Philadelphia

ISBN 978 1 39904 464 6

A CIP catalogue record for this book is
available from the British Library

Typeset by Mac Style
Printed in the UK by CPI Group (UK) Ltd, Croydon, CR0 4YY.

MIX
Paper | Supporting
responsible forestry
FSC® C013604

Pen & Sword Books Limited incorporates the imprints of After
the Battle, Atlas, Archaeology, Aviation, Discovery, Family History,
Fiction, History, Maritime, Military, Military Classics, Politics,
Select, Transport, True Crime, Air World, Frontline Publishing, Leo
Cooper, Remember When, Seaforth Publishing, The Praetorian Press,
Wharncliffe Local History, Wharncliffe Transport, Wharncliffe True
Crime and White Owl.

For a complete list of Pen & Sword titles please contact

PEN & SWORD BOOKS LIMITED
47 Church Street, Barnsley, South Yorkshire, S70 2AS, England
E-mail: enquiries@pen-and-sword.co.uk
Website: www.pen-and-sword.co.uk
or
PEN AND SWORD BOOKS
1950 Lawrence Rd, Havertown, PA 19083, USA
E-mail: uspen-and-sword@casematepublishers.com
Website: www.penandswordbooks.com

Dedicated to Grandma, who would have loved this book

Contents

Foreword

This is not a book about sex. This is a book about poor Victorian women living on the very edge of society. It is designed as an introduction to the world of Victorian prostitutes and can be used as a springboard for further research, a signpost to academic works and a door for family researchers unfamiliar with the lives of immoral women.

The women captured in these pages were vilified by their government and let down by abusive, violent and manipulative people, but through it all they lived colourful lives. It is still very much taboo to discuss prostitutes and prostitution, so this book opens the door to the lives of these Victorian women to show that their lived experiences are as relevant as anyone else's. These were women surviving in a cruel world with what little they had, which is something to which many women can still relate.

The writing for this book has been entirely carried out in the style of Florence Nightingale – from my bed. It is difficult to research and study when disabled, so this has been both a challenge and a delight. Any research has been carried out online, from my book collection, or from my MRes dissertation research, so there will be gaps. The focus of my dissertation was Victorian prostitutes in Stamford and Peterborough, and the women from these two locations feature heavily in the book. For this I make no apology: their lives were fascinating.

Notes

All fines referred to in the book are in pounds, shillings and pence – £ s d and follow the Victorian format. Likewise, the word jail is in the Victorian form of gaol.

All references to census, birth, marriage, burial and death records are from Ancestry.co.uk and Freereg.org.uk, except for the death certificates purchased from the General Register Office, and all newspaper records were sourced from The British Newspaper Archive. See the Bibliography section for more information.

Chapter 1

Falling: The Route into Prostitution

T o understand the life of a prostitute we must understand how she entered the life, or was handed the label. Her individual route into prostitution was based on specific circumstances in her life which forced or encouraged her down the route of immorality, and there was usually 'a multiplicity of reasons rather than a monocausal explanation' that led to her being known as a prostitute.[1] Some entered the life as girls and some as women; some continued in the life for many years and others flitted in and out again. Many used prostitution as a short-term solution to their money issues, or as a short period of teenage rebellion in a constrained society. The true number of women and girls working as prostitutes in the Victorian era will never be known, because a large proportion of the women who were selling sex, or enjoying sex outside of marriage, did not appear in police records or newspapers; those that did are the backbone of this book.

Girls

Having an unsecure and unsupported childhood was one of the biggest factors in a girl becoming a prostitute. This was something identified by commenters of the time including William Acton and Bracebridge Hemyng, and the work of Judith Walkowitz, Frances Finnegan and Linda Mahood.[2] Domestic violence, extreme poverty, abuse, and the death or loss of a parent were all significant factors in a girl becoming an 'unfortunate'. There is evidence of all of these childhood experiences throughout the book, some of which can be identified in the individual prostitute Life Stories set out through the book.

According to the *Leeds Mercury* in 1840, three quarters of girls who became prostitutes did so because of the following two reasons:

1. Having been servants in public houses or beer-shops, where they have been seduced by men frequenting those places of dissipation and temptation.
2. From the intermixture of the sexes in the factories.[3]

They put the fault in the hands of inscrutable employers and lusty men, and from the urges of the sexes working together in modern employment (see artwork on page X for a contemporary interpretation of the issue). What this fails to do is identify any issues or traumas in a girl's life that might lead her down an immoral path – the prostitute is the vessel here. The remaining quarter were again split, but this time into three groups:

1. Those who, being indolent or possessing bad tempers, leave their situations,
2. [Those who] have been driven to their awful course by young men *making false promises*…
3. Those who *by their own mothers* have been urged to become prostitutes for a living.

Bad tempers; bad choices; bad mothers! These reasons relate more to a childhood which would have helped to shape her temper, failed to protect her from the false promises of young men (or forgiven her for her mistakes), or indeed pushed her into prostitution. Many of the Victorian societies who set out to help prostitutes were acting to aid those *without* friends or family, because the young girls who were without either were much more vulnerable to exploitation and 'seduction' than others.

Parent Loss

A girl who had lost one or both parents was significantly more likely to have ended up in the workhouse and/or in a poverty-stricken household, particularly if it was her father who had died. The death of her father would have led her mother to look for work, which would not provide enough money to support the family (women were paid less than men for the same work) and could have led to her being absent from home for most of the day. This in turn would have forced older children to either care for the younger ones, or to be forced into work themselves, putting them in precarious and vulnerable positions and of course removing them from school and any possible chance of finding a better paid job in the future. They were unskilled, uneducated and unprotected.

Losing a mother left a girl without female guidance, which was Annie Casey's defence in 1868, when she admitted to dragging a man into a house in Sheffield where she beat and robbed him with another prostitute.[4] Annie (21) had grabbed Edwin Sykes by the wrists and pulled him into a house in Punch Bowl Yard. Once they were locked in the house she started beating him with a poker with her friend, Catherine Waring Glover. By the time they unlocked the door to the police, Edwin was a bloody, unconscious, mess on the floor. Annie claimed she hit his head and would have killed him. When he came round, Edwin realised that he was missing £4 and a ring from his finger worth £20. Annie claimed that she was 'a mother-less child', but had been well-behaved before then – which was a flagrant lie. She sobbed as she claimed that 'she had been a neglected child since she was nine years of age and had had nobody to look after her moral instruction or welfare'. Her words were written down as she begged forgiveness: 'Have mercy upon me this time ... and I will endeavour to do wrong no more.' The judge, reminding Annie that she had nearly killed Edwin, had not an ounce of sympathy and sent her to gaol for seven years.[5] Her words were just for show; she was involved in further criminal activity after her release from gaol, and after she married too.

Losing a father left a family without the major breadwinner. This pushed families to the edge and forced children into work at young ages, when they were vulnerable to exploitative employers and, if in service, the advances of fellow servants – and even their employer's children.

To lose both parents as a child was the greatest tragedy and usually resulted in the child ending up in the local workhouse. The Tingey sisters (see their Life Story) lost their mother first, then after their father became ill the whole family moved into the workhouse. He died there, the children having no choice but to grow up in the walls of the workhouse. For both Tingey sisters, their eventual escape from the workhouse was into a brothel. Elizabeth Ann Tremberth, who appears several times in this book, lost both of her parents before the age of 10. Born in Gwennap, Cornwall, towards the end of 1851, she was a late baby for her parents William and Catherine. Her father was, like many men in Cornwall, a miner. By the 1861 census when Elizabeth was 10, she was already living with her aunt, Mary Gidley – described as a gentlewoman – and her two older siblings James (20, a miner) and Catherine (18, a scholar). Her mother Catherine had died in January 1856 when Elizabeth was 4 years old, and her father remarried a year later. Sadly, he died in the January of 1859, leaving Elizabeth an orphan at the age of 8; thankfully, her aunt was also her next-door neighbour, so she didn't have to move far to her new home, and her stepmother was close by.

Despite losing her parents, Elizabeth had support around her and should have been in a comfortable position if her aunt was a gentlewoman. Elizabeth was not a typical friendless orphan dumped in a workhouse, but there must have been other issues in her life that led to her leaving home and living as a prostitute. She was a revolving-door criminal, getting little further than the gaol gates before being found guilty of vagrancy and being sent back in again.

Elizabeth's first sentence was in 1869 when she was 18.[6] Like most young people, she had moved to her nearest town, Redruth, to seek work and soon found herself in a desperate situation. We don't know how old she was when she left her family; it would be easy to assume that she could have remained in education until the age of 18, like her sister Catherine, but by that age she was already working the streets of Redruth. One thing to note about Elizabeth, however, is that she was described as having a speech impediment, so it is possible that she struggled to find work due to discrimination, and found the prostitute community of Redruth the most supportive. Her early experiences, and journey into prostitution, serve as a reminder that the knowledge we gain from documents can only flirt with the reality of a situation and, unless we're really lucky, it's usually impossible to know the many reasons that led a girl or woman down that path.

Parental Harm

Elizabeth Griggs of Bedford claimed that she had no choice but to become a prostitute 'as her mother neglected to maintain her'.[7] Elizabeth had been called up at the Borough Petty Sessions for being drunk and swearing in the streets in the afternoon, however that wasn't the full story. The real reason was that complaints had been made relating to her treatment of her younger half-sister, Harriet Hill. Elizabeth was 26, and Harriet only 13; Elizabeth had been dragging Harriet along by her hair and attempting to hit her. She was often unpleasant to her, frequently swearing, kicking and hitting her in the yard they shared with their neighbours. Their mother, Julia, lived with them but did nothing to help their situation. In the 1871 census Elizabeth was named as the head of the family and was working as a lacemaker, a common but poorly paid occupation for women in the area – but also a term synonymous with prostitution. Her sister Harriet was described as a servant, and their mother a laundress. What the census didn't record was that Elizabeth was heavily pregnant and gave birth to her son, William Henry, shortly after the census. By the time she went in front of the bench, his maintenance was given as another reason why she was working as a prostitute.

Elizabeth Ellen Cox's mother existed at the other end of the parenting scale and rather than leaving her daughter to her own travails, believed in beating the poor behaviour out of her. Elizabeth lived in Swindon, Wiltshire, and was working as a prostitute at the age of 16. She was accused of behaving indecently on Cricklade Road, information that was too indelicate to report in the papers. The police superintendent made the case that her mother had beaten her many times, 'but without the desired effect'.[8] She was sent to gaol for one month.

The child of a prostitute was likely to have been born without any knowledge of who their father was – unless their mother happened to marry them, and even then, if police reports and inquests are any indication, men who married prostitutes were not usually of the nurturing type. At the point of birth, if the child was fatherless and subject to poverty, shame and insults from wider society, they had no choice as they grew up but 'to regard themselves as social outcasts'.[9] It was usually impossible for mothers to protect their children from the world they inhabited, if indeed they wished to. Zella Wilkinson grew up in her mother's brothel in Louth, Lincolnshire. In October 1838, both mother and daughter appeared before the court: the mother, Elizabeth Wilkinson, was gaoled for a year for running a brothel; Zella received the same punishment for being a prostitute.[10] The passing on of this way of life from mother to daughter was, understandably, something that morality reformers were very concerned about, which is why laws were eventually updated in the 1880s and 1890s to clamp down on brothels and the children growing up in them.

Seducers

When a girl left home to look for work she was, at that point, independent, and there was an expectation that she would not return home. This was even more so for children leaving a single parent household, or kind relatives who had provided a temporary home, as we have already observed. It is therefore unsurprising that many girls who travelled for honest work accidentally found themselves living in a brothel, or duped into a less than desirable situation and had no ability to extricate themselves. Jane Billington of Preston claimed all of her troubles could be traced back to an Italian or German man named Peter Winter. Jane had ended up in Kendal, where she was charged with being a disorderly prostitute and being drunk and disorderly on Highgate in the early hours of the morning. She said that she had been 'enticed' from her home by Peter to play instruments with other girls.[11] He mistreated them and sent them off 'to the lowest brothels to lodge'. The arresting sergeant agreed with her statement, saying she was living in a small room with two other girls 'at one of the worst houses in town'. The brothel was being kept by a woman named Mary Sandwich, aka 'Old Moll/Mall Madge'.[12] Twenty-first century eyes reading that case would immediately expect Peter Winter and 'Mall Madge' to be arrested and for the three girls to be rescued, but this was not the reality of life in 1847. Jane was sentenced to a month in gaol for her behaviour. Peter Winter does not appear again in the newspapers, but 'Mall Madge' was charged with running a brothel a few months later, alongside her friend Elizabeth Slee.[13] They were described as having such a 'repulsive appearance' that they 'might be supposed to be "a terror to evil doers".' They didn't go to gaol, but agreed to 'go "to t' warkhouse"' instead.

Spending some of their childhood in the workhouse was also a good indicator that a girl would be labelled a prostitute as an adult. Girls were often encouraged into the lifestyle by prostitutes who had gone into the workhouse to give birth or recover from disease, or from brothel keepers who (it was claimed) would enter the workhouse specifically to recruit girls.

The life story of the Tingey girls reveals that both sisters went directly from the workhouse to a brothel, both finding themselves in a form of debt bondage. Being without family and respectable friends was (and still is) a significant factor in someone being misled into crime and/or a position of subordination or slavery.

Some girls who became prostitutes were born to respectable families and were supposedly brought up in 'decent' situations but were still identified as prostitutes. Emma Browning lived in Frome, Somerset, and at the age of 16 had been labelled as a prostitute. Her father, Thomas Browning, was described in the 1861 census as a confectioner and pastry cook, and also as blind.[14] Emma and her two brothers all attended school and they appeared to live in a decent street with equally hard-working neighbours. By the age of 14 Emma was working as a servant and that was when she received her first gaol time. She was charged under the Vagrancy Act with staying overnight in a privy and locked up for one calendar month.[15] There were a significant number of prostitutes who had initially worked as servants, and lost their innocence and their job. These women and girls were new to the world and were taken advantage of by employers and colleagues – but they also took advantage of their single female status too.

When she was 16, Emma was found 'lying about in the streets and having no visible means of subsistence'.[16] She was discharged on this occasion and was ordered to be sent back to her parents, but they refused to take her in – at the age of 16 she was on her own. With no support from her home, she headed instead to London and worked as a servant there. Curiously, she appeared in the baptismal records of St Mary the Virgin, Soho, in 1871, which was a terribly poor area but a very popular church.[17] Her baptism really stands out among the other baptisms due to her parents' address in Frome and her age – she was just shy of her nineteenth birthday. It is possible that she had found her way to a reformatory or well-wisher who encouraged her to find faith and cast off her immoral life.

Things didn't go as planned, and by 1881 she had slipped into the workhouse system. She had a little boy, Harry, on 17 November in Islington Workhouse Infirmary. They seemed to move between several workhouses and infirmaries immediately following his birth, with a suggestion that Harry was not a healthy baby. There doesn't appear to be a birth or death record for Harry, and given his start in life, it is very probable that he died in infancy. He did at least live long enough to appear in the 1881 census with Emma in Hackney Workhouse. Emma left the workhouse and began working again as a servant again – a cook – for a widow in Beckenham, possibly making use of her father's skills.

By 1897 Emma was 45 and married Thomas James Churchill, a bricklayer. Her marriage didn't yield any children, but it was a long one and they lived on a neat little terrace in Fulham. Emma died in 1926 in her 70s.

What Emma's story highlights is that not all women who were named as prostitutes had come from poor backgrounds, but working as a servant could open a door to an immoral life. It also shows that they were capable of escaping a life of crime and destitution, and this serves to remind us that London was not a festering cesspit of degradation for every prostitute who was drawn there; it was possible to find honest work and a decent husband.

Florence Stanley, 24, had also come from 'respectable parentage', but in August 1875 had been found drunk and disorderly on the streets of Stamford.[18] She had been living at the worst brothel in Stamford with the Tomblin family, and after a quarrel got very drunk indeed. She explained to the bench that she had lived a respectable life but her parents had disowned her 'in consequence of having lived for a time with a gentleman who was now in India'. There is no more information to explain whether the man was a soldier, a businessman, or just a liar (it was much easier to move to the other side of the country but claim you were moving to India), or indeed if she had been seduced, but without the man she loved or the support of her family, she was alone and desperate. She asked to enter the Penitent Home so that she could escape her life, but was instead sent to the workhouse as a holding pen while her parents were contacted (returning a daughter to her parents was much cheaper for the town than the expense of the Penitent Home).

Lily Ball had made the progression from prostitute to running a disorderly house when she went in front of the bench, but she blamed her poor conduct on her childhood. She was accused of running a disorderly house in Duston, Northamptonshire, in 1889, which carried a much heavier sentence than it had earlier in the century.[19] The police had been watching Lily's house and provided details about the number of men and women entering and leaving it, proving that Lily and her housemate, Lizzie Baker, were both living as prostitutes. Lily's defence claimed this was her first offence, and that she 'had had a most unfortunate career, being seduced when young under a promise of marriage, which was broken'. Lily had had a baby, but had enough help or foresight to be able to remove the child from her situation and place it in a boarding school, so it was 'free from contamination'. Hearing her story, the bench decided not to fine her the full £20 liable, but only £5 with 18s 6d costs.

Stories of seduction were common, with men promising young women marriage to persuade them to indulge in their carnal lust. A great deal of couples enjoyed a roll in the hay once they had promised to marry, and a considerable number of women walked down the aisle pregnant – but promises are only as good as the person who makes them; a soldier, sailor, or itinerant worker could say whatever he wished to 'bed' a woman and leave the next day without having to face the consequences. This was less common in small rural communities where everyone knew everyone else. When accidental pregnancies occurred the young couple could be forced to marry for the sake of respectability, or at the very least the man would be required to pay bastardy payments to the mother, which would help to keep her out of the workhouse or off the streets. In the tangle of constantly moving urban lives, it was much easier for a woman to be seduced and abandoned. It could be argued that greater mobility during the Industrial Revolution was a direct cause of the increase in seduction and abandonment, and therefore a growth in the number of abandoned women forced into prostitution. It could also be argued that women's increased mobility provided more opportunities to meet men who could seduce them.

The secretary of The London Female Preventive and Reformatory Institution wrote to local newspapers asking for support for the vast numbers of girls who had arrived in London and needed help. He claimed: 'seventy per cent of the unhappy creatures who crowd our streets have suffered their first fall through the wiles of the betrayers, thus losing their characters and their means of livelihood through one false step'.[20]

Abuse

For some women their route into prostitution had started with abuse at home. The need to escape from violence, physical and emotional abuse, neglect, sexual abuse, or a combination of them, forced women to leave home in search of something better – but they were ill-equipped to find it. Experiencing sexual assault as a small girl would have removed the mystery of sex and the preciousness of virginity that other girls grew up with. With the threads of morality already cut, there was nothing to stand in the way of them becoming prostitutes. This was not seduction but ravishing – a very serious crime, but with a less than satisfactory penalty.

Jane Marshall of Wisbech, Cambridgeshire was accused of stealing a purse in Stamford in 1865. She was 'on tramp' and had already walked to nearby Ketton in Rutland before she was caught. Jane was described as 'an abandoned character', but the truth was far worse.[21] Jane was born to William and Mary Marshall in 1842, but Mary sadly died when Jane was a baby. This left William with several young children to look after by himself, so he remarried in 1843, which resulted in the birth of his youngest daughter, Rose. His second wife, Ann, had also died by the time of the 1851 census, leaving him with five children still at home to care for.

In 1859 they were living in Walsoken, near Wisbech, when William raped Jane; she was 17. He had been attempting to assault her for a few weeks, which had led her to sleeping on the hearthrug fully clothed during the night.[22] He came home from the pub very drunk one night and forced himself on her, repeating the event the following night. Jane fled to a neighbour on the second night, who was then a credible witness to the scene. Jane was also examined and there were marks of violence on her.

Her father's defence was that Jane was lying and was 'an undutiful and unruly child and was in the habit of associating with bad companions'. He was found guilty of the crime and sentenced to fifteen years of penal servitude. By the 1861 census, Jane was living with a small group of women on the edge of Walsoken. They were all of a similar age to Jane and it is very likely to have been a brothel. Whether she was already friends with these women and they were the 'bad companions' her father referred to, or they were a supportive home to a traumatised teenager, we can only guess.

Women

Not all women became prostitutes because of their childhoods, and many older women were either labelled with the term due to their 'immoral' behaviour, or had resorted to prostitution due to their circumstances. William Logan was one of the figures calling for the repeal of the Contagious Diseases Acts (see Chapter 7) and through his work, combined with the knowledge of campaigners such as Josephine Butler, he became aware 'that the initial causes of women resorting to prostitution were overwhelmingly poverty, overcrowding and poor pay, working conditions and employment opportunities for women'.[23]

Due to women's pay being far lower than men's, it was often impossible for women to support a family on their meagre wages in the way a man could. Should a woman find herself alone due to her husband dying, being imprisoned, or abandoning her, she could very quickly find herself unable to meet her basic needs. Even if she could find work, she would probably need to supplement it to be able to pay her rent and eat. There were, therefore, a large number of women working casually as prostitutes to keep themselves alive; they had made a choice – but the two options were prostitution or destitution (potentially leading to death). These often stayed out of the newspapers, but they were witnessed by contemporaries writing about prostitutes. Prostitution was not an easy choice for those women, and 'prostitute' was not a name they would have used to describe themselves. Nor was it intended to be a permanent state; the aim of marrying or finding a better situation was always on their mind.

Esther Smith, alias Moloy, turned to prostitution after her husband died. In 1891 she was accused of running a brothel, by keeping another prostitute at her house in Nelson Street, Maryport, Cumbria. She denied the charge, but Sergeant Simon claimed that he 'could testify that Esther had been living a very immoral life since her husband died two years ago'.[24] Likewise Rebecca Liddell had turned to prostitution in Jarrow after her husband left. She hadn't appeared before the courts before and was treated lightly, despite being seen to stop three men in North Street.[25] When Jane Morris was arrested on the streets of Birmingham in 1886, she was observed to be new to the life and was asked by Alderman Manton 'if she would be willing to leave the life she had lately begun'.[26] In response she 'said she could not do so, for she had a husband who was ill with rheumatic fever and for whom there was nothing else she could do'. The money she earnt from her prostitution was the only thing keeping her family alive.

Older women who had been running homes and/or had children were more likely to move into brothel-keeping than prostitution. Because they were more likely to have a home and needed lodgers to pay the rent, taking on prostitutes meant they could also earn money from their lodgers and so maintain a familiar home for their children. This is one of the reasons that fewer older women worked as prostitutes, as the next chapter will reveal.

There were many routes into prostitution, and usually a key event or failure that led to young lives being destroyed or older lives being upended. But there was also some help provided by the church, organisations for the protection of girls, and sympathy from the court system. And, as the life of Emma Browning demonstrates, it was entirely possible to find your way out of prostitution too.

Life Story: Catherine Thirkettle

Great Yarmouth's position on the east Norfolk coast at the mouth of the rivers Yare, Waveney and Bure, was the perfect place to load and unload goods to and from Norwich and Europe and had been for centuries. The town had always had a distinct maritime identity and, as the Victorian census shows, was both a permanent and temporary home to a large contingency of sailors, mariners and fishermen crossing the North Sea. Once the railway arrived in the 1840s, goods could be transported with greater ease from the town, bypassing the winding river routes, but the town maintained its maritime identity. The arrival of the railway also introduced holidaymakers to the town, lured by Yarmouth's picturesque long sandy beaches and fresh air, features that still draw visitors today.

For centuries, Yarmouth had been confined to the medieval imprint of the town with the rich and the poor muddled together in incredibly narrow streets known as the Rows (see image on page X). The Rows ran roughly east to west, and the vast majority were named after a person or pub, sounding like something from a children's book, e.g., Page the Pipe Maker's Row, and Haynes the Peruke Maker's Row. The array of often-confusing names led to them being numbered at the beginning of the nineteenth century.

Despite the width of some of the streets in the Rows being less than a metre wide in places, they were in use long after other towns had widened and improved their medieval streets. They remained an integral part of the lives of the people in Victorian Great Yarmouth, even after the building of spacious new streets to the north. It was in these historic narrow streets that our subject grew up.

Catherine Thirkettle was born Elizabeth Catherine Thirkettle in Great Yarmouth on 2 May 1859, and baptised at St Nicholas' Church on 20 May. Her parents were named Robert and Isabella, and met when they were teenagers and both living in Row 1 (also known as Rampart Row). In the 1851 census, Isabella was lodging with the Thirkettles before her marriage to Robert in 1852; she was working as a braider, almost certainly of fishing nets; Robert worked as a sawyer, like his father.

Robert and Isabella's first child, Martha, was born in January 1854 but not baptised until March 1855 at St Nicholas' Great Yarmouth. She died a month later, along with a Sarah Thirkettle, suggesting that illness had struck the family and they were afraid that Martha would die and not go to heaven. At the time of her baptism Robert's occupation was given as a 'militiaman', telling us that he had joined the East Norfolk Militia, which had a large garrison in the town. The Crimean War was in its second year and a large number of men had been persuaded to sign up as reservist soldiers. Even though he would not have been to war, Robert would no doubt have been proud of his role in the militia and representing his town.

Martha Mary Ann, known as Mary Ann, was born just after the end of the war in 1856, by which time Robert had taken on his father's business after his death. Catherine was their third and final child, born three years later in 1859.

Death was never far away from the Thirkettles and in June 1864 Catherine's mother died, aged 41, in Yarmouth workhouse from 'febris', or fever. Catherine was only 5 years old at the time. Her father's death followed a few years after that; he also died in the workhouse, tragically from 'paralysis'. His occupation was not recorded as a sawyer at the time of his death, but as a bricklayer's labourer, which might provide an explanation for how he had come to be paralysed.[27] Catherine was an orphan at the age of only 8, but it's very likely she was taken in by her wider family. By the 1871 census her sister Mary Ann was living with their grandmother Sarah, and aunt and uncle Archer, but Catherine, then aged 11, has so far proved elusive in the census records, not appearing in the workhouse, or with close relatives.

We do know that she remained living in Great Yarmouth and lived out her messy teenage years in the Rows. The first clue to her immoral life was in 1874 when she was identified as a disorderly prostitute under the name Kitty Thirkettle; she was barely 15.[28] She was found to be drunk in the streets and fined 5s. In the following year she was arrested for fighting in the Rows and 'using the most frightful language'.[29] As a policeman attempted to take her to the police station, she threw herself to the ground and later attempted to bite him! She was sentenced to a month in gaol, which would have meant a journey to the County Gaol in Norwich Castle, the old gaol in Great Yarmouth being only recently made redundant from its role.

At the time of her arrest a rescue attempt was made by a man named Joseph Barber, who jumped to her defence; he also found himself in front of the bench and was landed with a 10s fine. Joseph and Catherine were very likely related through the marriage of her sister Mary Ann to George Barber, indicating that family ties were important to them.

By the 1881 census Catherine was 21 and living with a boarder on Row 31, also known as Nine Parish Row. She was acknowledged as the head of the household and as a young single woman you might expect the boarder to be of a lower status, perhaps another woman, another prostitute, or a transient man – one of the many fishermen, sailors, or smacksmen passing through the town looking for a bed for the night. However, her boarder was Carl August Hanson, a sailor from Gothenburg, Sweden, and he was anything but a transient sailor.

On 27 August 1882 Catherine and Carl married at St Nicholas' Church. Curiously, they had their banns read first on three consecutive Sundays in January 1882, with the earliest document relating to their banns dating to 31 December 1881, nearly ten months before they actually married. We know from this document that they were living on Row 30, Barnaby the Baker's Row, close to where they had been living at the time of the census. At first, Carl claimed to be living with 'E C Thirkettle', but this had been crossed out and replaced by Mrs Scagar/Seagar, who had accompanied Catherine to sign the banns certificate. Carl had supposedly been living there for eight months and Catherine for one day. The name of Carl's father is not given, and 'a swede' is written underneath the 'Name' box. After their banns being read in St Nicholas' Church on three consecutive Sundays, the expectation would be for them to marry straight after, but they did not. Perhaps they argued or perhaps there was an impediment – perhaps Carl had to head back to Sweden.

Whatever the issue, they overcame it and they had their banns read again in August. The first, on 11 August, tell us that the couple had been living with Catherine's aunt, 'Mrs Thirkettle', on Nelson Road. It was she who went with them to sign their banns for the second time. Catherine's uncle Nathaniel Thirkettle and aunt, Rachel Thirkettle, were witnesses at the wedding, so it was very likely that Rachel was the 'Mrs Thirkettle' she claimed to be living with.

The document also tells us that Carl claimed he had been living in Yarmouth for seven years and with Catherine her whole life, but they had been together for five years, which is quite different to the original declaration. This means Catherine would have been 18 when she started her relationship with Carl in 1877 and raises the question of whether they were cohabiting, with Catherine supporting herself with prostitution while he was away, or she would have identified herself as a sailor's wife and depended on his income. Once she was in a relationship with Carl she appears to have stayed out of the papers, other than as a victim, suggesting there was some stability in her life when she was with him. However, the fact that it took five years for them to marry and they pushed back the wedding would suggest that their relationship was not the safe haven it could have been.

In a typical Victorian marriage we would expect to see a few children born, but there are no records of any. This could be due to being too poor to baptise them or, as was common with many prostitutes, that no children were born to them. Prostitutes were known to have had a lower birth rate, with many failing to produce any offspring at all, partly due to venereal disease, miscarriage and also early infant mortality.[30]

Tragically, their marriage ended after only five years, with Catherine following her parents to an early death in the workhouse. She died in January 1888 in Great Yarmouth workhouse at the age of 28 and was buried in Yarmouth New Cemetery on 31 January. She had 'phthisis', which we now know as tuberculosis, and would have had a slow, painful death (see death certificate on page X), potentially over many years.

Carl had not been a loyal and supportive husband; online records show that he had been living a double life, such was the privilege of the dual-home sailor. He had returned to Sweden shortly after his marriage to Catherine and only two years later he had started a family with another woman in 1884, having fathered two boys before Catherine's death.

There are plenty of notes to take away from Catherine's short life. First, poverty and disease were at the heart of this story, with Catherine and her parents all dying in the workhouse at a young age. Second, it is a reminder that becoming an orphan in the Victorian period significantly increased your likelihood of becoming a prostitute. The combination of poverty and lack of parental guidance and support united a great number of the women who entered the trade. Third, Catherine lived her entire life in the confines of Great Yarmouth, almost never moving outside of its densely packed streets. In contrast, her sailor husband was travelling the world and was able to start a new relationship in his home country while she lay dying. Women were hugely restricted by what they could do and where they could go, often reliant on whatever or whoever fell at their feet. Carl must have seemed an exciting opportunity when he first appeared in Catherine's life, but he gave her nothing more than a signature on a marriage certificate and a life of regret.

Chapter 2

Their Tawdry Finery:
What Prostitutes Looked Like

Clothing

The majority of the women discussed in this book are from the poorest level of society; some were filthy wretches, but most conformed to society's expectations of what a woman should look like. At their most basic, they had long hair, wore a corset, boots, skirt or dress, and put on a hat when they went out. For those women who were part-time prostitutes, working to top-up their meagre wages, they would have blended with the other women around them. Those labelled prostitutes because they weren't living with their husbands, or were living with men they weren't married to, also looked the same.

This contrasts with Medieval and Early Modern prostitutes who were often forced to identify themselves by wearing very specific outfits. The constant battle to control prostitution in towns led to both their homes and clothing being regulated. Medieval sumptuary laws around Europe restricted the way a prostitute could dress, by providing strict rules about what must or must not be worn. For example, striped hoods were forced upon prostitutes in a few locations in England in the fourteenth century to separate them from other classes. In London, the wearing of fur and lambswool by prostitutes was forbidden, and those of the lower classes too. Prostitutes earning good money might have been in a position to buy expensive clothes and advance themselves in circles above their original situation (see Susan Tingey's Life Story), but these laws prevented that from happening and forced women to dress appropriately for their class.

By the nineteenth century these rules had vanished, but the ideology remained. The moral outrage at the perceived infestation of prostitutes in the country flamed the idea that prostitutes were a separate class of women who could be identified by appearance alone. Their clothing choices were thought to be immoral, and a visual sign of the degraded lives they lived, just as they had been for the prostitutes who came before them. People looked to the newspapers to inform them what prostitutes looked like in order to avoid them; they needed to know that the villain or the victim in news reports was dressed as per the caricature in their head. These descriptions matched the gaudy images of prostitutes in satirical images and cartoons, thus ensuring that the left and right hand were in agreement: prostitutes were vulgar, and legitimate source of ridicule.

Some Victorian prostitutes were as visible as the medieval prostitutes of the sumptuary laws, but instead of being forced into distinctive clothing, they wore it for fashion, for a sense of belonging, or just for fun. In Chesterfield there was a reference to 'pink flounced ladies' in 1859 by Reverend J. Hanson.[1] Flounced skirts were very popular at the time and his comment suggests that several of the prostitutes who met in The Swan in Chesterfield wore them in a fetching shade of pink – perhaps to identify themselves as prostitutes, or simply as a sign of friendship; whichever it was (for an example of flounced skirts see page X), the Reverend Hanson grouped and classified these women as prostitutes based on their choice of skirts.

Certainly, the pink flounced ladies might have looked rather gaudy in a public house, but prostitutes weren't all dressed in such a flamboyant manner. Images of prostitutes placed in Repeat Offender books show many weathered and poorly dressed souls who would have been happy for a clean skirt, let alone a flounce. But the press' infatuation with and comments on women's dress and style never waned.

At a gathering of young people in pubs, beerhouses and lodging houses in Leeds, 'the prostitutes were easily distinguished from the factory girls by their tawdry finery and the bareness of their necks'.[2] This account had been written by Mr Symons in 1843, a commissioner of the Children's Employment Commission who was horrified at the large number of youths drinking in establishments late at night. He reported that prostitutes and factory girls mixed freely with the young men, and that the factory girls' dress was 'not altogether dissimilar' to the prostitutes. It was the bare necks of the prostitutes – their tantalising flesh – that really stood them apart.

Elizabeth Roberts is one of the few prostitutes where an attempt was made to recreate her image in the papers. She was in her mid-20s when she appeared in court in 1883 for attempting to kill her little girl in Chester. She was described as 'a young woman of repulsive appearance', and 'a loose character' who was an angry drunk and was particularly unpleasant to her 14-month-old daughter, Sarah Ann.[3] The *Illustrated Police News* shared an artist's impression of the violent scene on the front page. She was described as 'a rather sullen-looking woman', and was 'wearing a black dress, with a white handkerchief tied loosely around her neck'.[4] In the imagined scene Elizabeth appeared in a black dress with a white handkerchief, swinging her infant daughter by her ankle; a clue to her profession was given in the glimpse of white stocking or bare skin under her skirt. The high-necked dresses of her horrified companions make it appear as if they were all virtuous ladies taking tea and Elizabeth the only prostitute. This was far from the truth, but the artist was creating an image to increase newspaper sales, and the scene is one of high drama.

Some prostitutes would dress well to appear more attractive to clients, but this was met with by scorn by many, who relied on the popular caricatures for their information (see page X for an example). Margaret Brown of Whitehaven spent two nights in the town lock-up in 1864, and it was said that her 'general appearance, enhanced as it might once have been by various adornments in the shape of [a] hat and feathers, was by no means improved by two nights incarceration'.[5] Such a description would have come from the journalist who was sitting in court and fed the belief that prostitutes were ugly, even with adornments.

Of course, some of the prostitutes did behave horrendously, with no care for their reputation or the way they looked. The nameless prostitute who was asleep in the King's Head in Coleford, Gloucestershire, in October 1857, was lying on the settle next to a man who was also asleep.[6] She was so drunk that her head 'hung over the end of the settle, her knees were up and her person exposed'.[7] Thankfully, the witness covered over her modesty. At that time women's drawers were split, rather than closed, so it would have been quite easy to expose herself if her skirts were raised. Had she been sleeping like that in the street, she would have been arrested.

What's in a Name?

Using newspapers as the main source of information to identify what prostitutes looked like has its issues, namely that there weren't many pictures and the language used to describe and label prostitutes was particularly pejorative. Photography was a new invention in the nineteenth century and it took a long time before photographs started appearing in newspapers. Photographs that do exist are largely from criminal records – Repeat Offender books, Prison Registration books and the like. But even then, images of prostitutes from police records give us a snapshot of defiance or misery, not the real essence of the women.

Newspapers often shied away from naming women as prostitutes, preferring to skirt around a word considered unseemly and unsuitable for delicate eyes or ears.[8] The term 'unfortunate' was frequently used, along with being a member of the 'frail sisterhood'; other descriptors included women 'of easy virtue', and a woman in Norwich who was described as being of 'frail reputation'.[9] These terms elicited sympathy, but would also have painted a picture of weak, ill-looking wretches. Some were simply referred to as 'representatives of a/their class', the 'social evil', or, when reporting a second prostitute story, 'ladies of the same stamp', again separating them from other women in society and grouping them as the same genus – a sub-genus of women below all others. The 'lost and erring daughters of Eve', frames the women in a religious context and as a group of women who could potentially be saved from their lives – as much sinned against as sinning. This contrasted with the term 'Cyprians', which was used as yet another general term for prostitutes, the word being associated with Aphrodite, the Greek goddess of love and patron goddess of prostitutes, and her cult in Cyprus.

Some of the descriptors were locators, the most famous being 'ladies of the pavement', or one of its many variations.[10] 'Women of the town' and 'night walkers' were also common monikers, making something of the fact that these women worked the streets at night when women of any respectable background knew to stay at home or travel by carriage at night. Some were more specific, relating to a street or pub, with prostitutes in Leighton Buzzard known as 'North End Vixens', and in Huddersfield known as the 'nymphs of Castlegate'.[11]

There was a wide array of personal signifiers in use to describe prostitutes, from the unimaginative to the unpleasant. Prostitute nicknames found across the country included:

Fat Liz
Big Nance
Gipsy Charlotte
One-eyed Liz
Coal-rake Nan
Sall the Rag
Curly
The Cheese Cutter
Opera Bet
The Creature Rudkin
Grimy Smith
Zulu
Little Jeannie
Swallow
Yankee (an American)
The Flying, Fiery Pheasant

Other women chose names to supposedly elevate their status or avoid detection; Jane Brattey was also known as Lady Godiva, possibly a reference to her long hair or regular nakedness. Wraysbury Hannah was also known as 'Sergeant Major', and of all of the women living in the Windsor brothel she called home, she was the 'noisiest woman of the lot'.[12]

Physical Characteristics

Police and court records often recorded the physical characteristics of people going through the system. This acted as a means of identifying the person if they appeared again in that location, or elsewhere in the system. Hair and eye colour, height, weight, scars and tattoos were all detailed, and occasionally, there are photographs too. Elizabeth Faulkner, a Cheltenham prostitute, was an inveterate thief and violent woman. She plagued Cheltenham for several years until she was transported in 1866 for seven years. At her first visit to Gloucester Gaol, she was described as having brown hair and eyes, a round face, a dark complexion (the other option being 'fresh') and being 4ft 11in tall (the average height of a woman at the time was 5ft 2in).[13] She had a 'scar on [the] thick of [her] left arm', and two moles on her neck. She was also described as stout.[14] The vast majority of women were described as having brown hair, with exceptions including older women who had grey hair. Elizabeth Ashworth of Peterborough, another violent woman, had a fresh complexion, brown eyes, grey hair (she was 43) and she too was described as stout.[15] A photograph of her accompanied the description and she is indeed a well-built woman. In the photograph of her on page X she looks back at the camera with a stare that the scant description failed to capture. She has a Trunchbull-esque stance and looks as if her life has been one of hardship and violence, something her criminal career attested to.

Annie Casey was a diminutive 4ft 8in (two inches shorter than Queen Victoria, who was considered short herself) with dark brown hair, a fair complexion and 'T H' tattooed above her left elbow. Initials were a common choice for tattoos at the time for both men and women. She was one of several women recorded in the Register of Female Prisoners at Wakefield Gaol with initials close to their elbows or wrists. The idea of tattooing a woman's body 'flouted Victorian ideals of feminine purity and decorum', and was associated with '[p]erceptions of tattooed women as sexually promiscuous and lower class'.[16] The initials suggest much more strongly that the tattoos were created to represent a loved one and that the body art was an act of love or devotion; an act that could only be associated with a woman who had already cast off the Victorian ideals of what a woman could or should do.

Disability was not uncommon. Sophie Preece of Hereford described herself as a cripple, the word also being used to describe a woman named Stanton of Cheltenham.[17] Ann Dunn of Wolverhampton was an old offender who had 'lost the use of her right hand'.[18] Despite this, she had still managed to pickpocket a man of a couple of sovereigns. Speech impediments were referenced in gaol registers, with Elizabeth Ann Tremberth from Gwennap, Cornwall, identified with the phrase 'impediment in speech'.[19] Frances Finnegan's work on York prostitutes also identified women who had entered the local penitentiary identified as having 'limited intelligence'.[20] Physical and cognitive disabilities were not treated with the knowledge and compassion of the twenty-first century, and for those who were perhaps unable to find work and/or safe relationships, the money they could earn, or steal, from prostitution, was the one thing keeping them from the workhouse or starvation.

Colour

Victorian prostitutes came in all sizes, shapes and skin tones. Those with an African or Asian heritage can be really difficult to identify in the records due to either a lack of information about ethnicity, or to misleading names, nicknames, or descriptions.

The colour of a woman's skin was information that was rarely offered in newspaper records. Just as the label prostitute was often only attached to a woman behaving immorally, the colour of the woman's skin was often only included when she was behaving in a particular way. There are some excellent books on the subject and *Black Victorians: Hidden in History* is an excellent starting point.[21]

Age

Some of the more critical Victorian accounts of prostitution, particularly those from London, would lead people to believe that most prostitutes were decoyed from their homes aged 13 and died a few years later, diseased and broken, but that simply wasn't representative of Victorian prostitutes. As the previous chapter showed, the reasons for women becoming prostitutes varied, and so did their entry into prostitution.

However, finding the ages of prostitutes in the newspapers is a challenge because they were often omitted. Older women were often referred to as 'old offenders' and young girls as girls and youths. The women themselves were also quite capable of lying about their age, as the life of Rosy Clarke attested to (see Life Story), or were just guessing their age, because they weren't sure themselves. Police records with prostitutes' ages were only as good as the word of the prostitute too, and were often inconsistent with women even lowering or maintaining their age over several years.

The majority of Victorian prostitutes were women in their late teens and early twenties. They were independent of their parents but not yet married. Because rates of pay were so poor for women, many had no choice but to supplement their income through sex work. They often only worked as prostitutes for a short while, having a singular black mark against their name as a prostitute before marrying, or finding another route out of prostitution. There were far fewer women working as prostitutes into their thirties. Older women identified included those who had been widowed or abandoned by their husbands, but they often moved into brothel-keeping and/or procuring, and so the prostitute label was dropped in favour of brothel keeper or procuress.

Whereas the vast majority of women stopped selling sex after a short while, others remained in the trade, or at least kept the label they had been given. Newspaper records show that some women were labelled as prostitutes into their 50s; this doesn't necessarily mean they were selling sex, but that they were behaving in a drunken, violent, or immoral way, and *looked* like a prostitute.

Using written sources to discover what Victorian prostitutes looked like is a challenge, but there are some rich and unexpected descriptions available. Analysing names provides clues to what women looked like, and along with descriptions of their clothing, hair, ages and heights, we can start to bring the image of Victorian prostitutes into better clarity. But every woman was an individual – there was no 'one size fits all' description of a Victorian prostitute. Her pink flounces or tattoos were her choice, and her expression of who she was; these choices and expressions were denied to many women higher up in society, so there were some benefits to living an immoral and ungoverned life.

Chapter 3

Reputation

The worst insult to a Victorian woman's morality was to be labelled a prostitute. A desperately poor woman on the verge of death from lack of food was held as morally superior to the woman who offered her body to pay for food to keep her children alive; the dead poor woman was going to heaven, and the prostitute would be eternally damned. This was Victorian England, the land of moral dichotomies: to be a prostitute was a sin, but to use one was okay. The poorest women in society were expendable, and as long as the man went home to his wife/family/battalion without any trouble, all was good with the world.

Prostitutes were said to spread diseases, moral discord and were a danger to the lives of other people. Each prostitute was 'made an outcast by the Victorian code of purity' that demanded respectable women were virtuous and only had sex with their husbands.[1] This often left prostitutes confined to a harsh underworld of crime, rejected from decent society and thought by many as no better than 'human residue'.[2]

The term prostitute didn't just apply to women who were selling sex, but could apply to any woman who slept with a man they weren't married to. The Victorian mentality was that '[a]ny woman contaminated by fornication was put practically on a level with the professional harlot'.[3] For a woman to be caught sleeping with a man other than her husband, or outside of an engagement, it could be nothing less than reputational suicide, leading to stigma and unfair treatment in court cases.

Bad Characters

Elizabeth Leslie of Warrington was the victim of an assault by James Brown in Warrington. The assault consisted of James running up to her, lifting up her clothes and hitting her in the face, which caused her to fall to the ground; he ran off. It was a simple case of unprovoked assault, but this was 1862, so Elizabeth's reputation was called into question during James' assault trail. She claimed she was a fustian cutter (a specialised job to cut the looped weft of thick cotton fabric to create, for example, corduroy) and did not consider herself a prostitute. 'I have not been "on the town" for several years, but I know I have not done right, as many a one beside me,' she said.[4] She appears to have been at no fault in the case and suffered a broken nose with collapsed cartilage, concussion, bruising and scars caused by her collapse. Her landlady described her nose being 'flattened upon her cheek' when she was returned home, but also stated she didn't know if Elizabeth lived entirely on prostitution, but she'd never seen her go to work. James' lawyer was the man to remind the jury that Elizabeth 'although a prostitute, was entitled to the same protection as any other person'. The jury decided that James was guilty, but due to his previous good behaviour and 'being of opinion that it was not his intention to have so severely injured the complainant', he was fined £5 or two months' hard labour in default. Had Elizabeth not been a prostitute, would he have received a greater punishment? Only the jury can answer that.

The idea that prostitutes had been born bad, or chosen to live immoral lives, set them apart from the higher classes who often regarded them as inhuman – or certainly lesser humans – that they could moralise and condemn. Whereas higher-class women needed protecting from all the evils in the world, 'the dangerous woman, in need of regulation and containment, came from the ranks of the poor and labouring classes'.[5] The work of physician William Acton aimed to change this view of prostitutes by considering how they found their way into prostitution and what could be done to support them. His views entered the public discourse and this led to some people questioning laws and the treatment of prostitutes.

In Liverpool, in January 1868, during the time of the Contagious Diseases Acts (see Chapter 7) a case was brought by John Dolsen against the magistrates. He was a landlord in Mersey Street, Liverpool, and had been fined for 'knowingly permitting persons of notoriously bad character to assemble'.[6] He argued that it was reasonable to allow prostitutes to use the premises 'to procure refreshments', but not 'in furthering of their calling as a prostitute'.

A prostitute had been 'classed as a person of notoriously bad character' in the Penal Servitude Amendment Act, yet the recorder, Mr J.B. Aspinall QC, 'said he entertained some doubts as to whether in this act of Parliament prostitutes could be found to be notoriously bad characters.'[7] He considered it entirely possible that the women were there for refreshment; the fact that they were drinking there with men did not mean that they were looking for clients. He could not find evidence that they were assembled for prostitution and quashed the previous conviction. He also made the comparison with thieves and argued that, 'if they found twenty or thirty notorious thieves sitting talking together, there was a reasonable inference they were arranging robberies', but it was not true to say that the same number of prostitutes gathered together had done so for the purposes of prostitution, for they might just have been drinking.[8]

Some could argue this was a brave move, for 1868 was at a time when public sentiment towards prostitutes was condemnatory, and Mr Aspinall may well have faced backlash for taking such a pragmatic and, some could argue, compassionate view of the women's habits. To view them as women seeking refreshments and not through blinkered eyes as 'bad characters' out to cause a nuisance goes very much against the purpose of the laws which unfairly targeted poor women. There were voices already speaking out in defiance of the Contagious Diseases Acts, but Josephine Butler's public campaign to repeal the laws didn't start until 1869.

Rape Accusations

Once named as a prostitute, it could be very difficult for a woman to cut the label from her neck. This meant that women who found themselves in court years after starting a new life could still find their integrity called into question after suffering horrific abuse. This was the case for Elizabeth Harrison, the wife of the station master at Chigwell Lane Station (now Debden tube station) in Debden, Essex, who claimed in 1867 that she was raped by their doctor.[9] He had previously taken liberties with Elizabeth, kissing her several times and telling her he loved her. She had told her husband and they had organised a summons, which had been met with a writ for slandering Dr Saunders.

The case was heard at Epping Petty Sessions. Elizabeth described how Dr Saunders had assaulted her in her bedroom, stopped the servant from entering the room and had attempted to pacify Elizabeth by repeating the words 'hush' and 'don't'. He offered to take her to London to the theatre to placate her. She complained to her husband and then set off to speak to Mrs Saunders, his wife. Mrs Saunders did not believe Elizabeth, stating he 'has had ten years of practice and I never heard a word against him before'. Dr Saunders called at the Harrison's house that evening with Rev. Meadows, the vicar of Chigwell. He told her it was a very serious charge and that he didn't believe her, it being 'a moral impossibility'. In prophetic and slightly threatening undertones, he told her: 'if you go on with this charge then it will be much worse for you'. Elizabeth stayed that night with friends who witnessed the marks on her body from her ordeal.

Dr Saunders' defence lawyer destroyed Elizabeth's character, accusing her of previously complaining about being assaulted in a railway carriage by a man putting his hand up her clothes. He then asked her where she met her husband. She admitted to meeting him in Peterborough, but refused to say how long she was there for or what she was doing. She was asked directly if she was a prostitute in Peterborough, which she denied, but still refused to state what her employment was. Mr Sleigh, her prosecution lawyer urged that he could not continue the case if she was refusing to answer questions put to her. Through very measured questioning she admitted to working as a dressmaker and that she knew 'Irish Car', but would not say if she lived with her. After her continual refusals to answer the questions set to her, her lawyer decided he could no longer represent her and he withdrew from the prosecution. His closing statement called into question his efficacy as Elizabeth's legal representative. He stated:

I consider that, as a prosecuting counsel in this case, a deep feeling of responsibility would rest upon me if a gentleman of respectability – which can be vouched upon by gentlemen now in the court – were kept for a moment longer in pain, suspense, or ignominy on the testimony of a person who had conducted herself in such a manner.

When the prosecutrix comes to the court and charges Mr Saunders with rape and afterwards refuses to answer any questions, then I say that she is not a person on whose testimony I can ask the justices to act. I have endeavoured to conduct this case with propriety and in a manner worthy of the position I have the honour to hold and I cannot do better in upholding my profession than by withdrawing from this prosecution. [Loud cheers in court].

The men involved in the case all shared in a celebratory backslapping at discrediting Mrs Harrison and entirely exonerating Dr Saunders. Let's be clear here: the case against Dr Saunders collapsed because Elizabeth refused to answer irrelevant questions about her past, not because she was unclear about the assault, nor about her corroborating witnesses, or her bruises. This case was held in front of magistrates who could not make a judgement of guilt on the doctor; the job of the magistrates at this point was to decide if the case had enough evidence to send it to a Grand Jury or to dismiss it for a lack of evidence. Instead, a boys' club mentality meant Elizabeth's own prosecutor withdrew for spurious reasons.

What makes this case even worse was that a ballad was created about the case.[10] In *The Ballad of the Stationmaster's Wife from Chigwell Road*, Elizabeth is painted as a 'false screaming woman' who 'refused to say one word about her former course of life', and who should really be in prison. She's painted as a profligate liar and Dr Saunders as a 'kind and skilful man' who was rightly exonerated from the case. For anyone who has watched a celebrity court case play out through social media this situation might seem familiar. The very idea of an esteemed man being guilty of such an immoral offence is unthinkable for the people who admire him. But the potential for a lesser person – in this case a perceived prostitute – to be lying for personal gain or revenge is much more acceptable. Confirmation bias, a powerful and blinkered state, entirely dominated this case, meaning Elizabeth did not get a fair trial and has had a tarnished name for the last 150 years. To have the hint of a stain on her reputation meant that there would only ever be one conclusion to the case, and it would never be in Elizabeth's favour.

The charge of rape was occasionally brought about by prostitutes, but it was very difficult to get a conviction for any woman who had been assaulted, let alone a woman who was known as a prostitute. Ann Waters brought an assault charge against seven men in 1848 when she was only 14. She was at Elvet Engine House, Durham, between 10 and 11 o'clock in the evening, which was an area known for prostitution, where she was assaulted by the young men. The case did not proceed due to lack of evidence, but the men received 'a reprimand from the bench for their disgraceful conduct'.

This came six years after an horrific attack on Margaret Jane Green on Blyth Sands, Durham, in front of a crowd of people. She had gone to Blyth beach with her friends on Sunday, 14 August 1842, the day before the Blyth Sands horseracing took place. Tents were pitched on the beach where local publicans sold their wares to working-class people enjoying a summer's day out with their friends and family.

Margaret was on the beach near the sand dunes when she was assaulted. Much of the case hinged around whether she was drunk or not – basically, whether or not it was her fault that she was gang raped in front of a crowd in the sand dunes. Three men, aged 18, 28 and 33, were accused of raping her, and two other men, aged 17 and 19, with assisting the others. There were two men working in Margaret's legal team, Mr Temple and Mr Otter, and in the course of their prosecution, they raised the issue of her being called a prostitute. 'She is entitled to the protection of the law,'[11] Mr Temple reminded the jury. 'A rape committed upon her person, without her consent, is quite as much of an offence against the law, as if she had been the purest person living. He pre-empted the jury bias against her status as a prostitute and asked them to look to the evidence of corroborating witnesses that proved her trustworthiness. He repeated this in regard to the question of whether she was likely drunk or not, asking them to consider that 'if she was in liquor, she was more likely to be deceived as to what was going on'. He emphasised the crowd of people surrounding the attack and questioned why no one intervened, stating: 'it speaks little for the state of morality among the common people in this part of the country'.

The case was very thorough in both collecting and reporting evidence. We know that the accused were taken to see Margaret after the attack, as she slipped in and out of hysteria, in order that she could identify them. We know that she was subjected to a doctor's examination where she was said to be showing evidence of 'inflammation of the bowels', as well as 'contusions' on her thighs and legs, swelling on her wrists and ankles, and some swelling internally. The defending lawyer claimed her inflamed bowels could have been caused by excessive drinking (see Chapter 10), and that the marks upon her body would have been greater if she had been held down; he suggested she had willingly taken part in the activities, not forcefully.

In summing up, the judge reminded the jury of the lawyer's request that she be treated fairly, regardless of whether she was drunk or a prostitute, but pointed out the many contradictions in witness statements. The jury retired for FIVE minutes. The 28- and 33-year-old men were found guilty, and the other three acquitted. The judge reminded the two guilty men that two years earlier they would have been executed for their crime. Instead, they were transported for life. The 33-year-old left behind a wife and four children.[12]

It is an interesting postscript to add that in 'a further proof of the perverse depravity of certain classes', Margaret had to be protected by three or four policemen on her way home after the trial. She was mobbed and 'loaded with opprobrious names'[13] as she fled to the inn at which she was staying, and the journalist feared she would have received physical violence had she not been protected. It is also worth noting that the *Durham Chronicle* was a four-page paper, and this story spread across three of those pages, such was the detail of the information reported.

Health Care and Support

The view that prostitutes were solely responsible for spreading disfiguring sexual diseases throughout the armed services via their lusty endeavours was entrenched in public opinion. Prostitutes were thought a blight on neighbourhoods, a corrupting influence, and riddled with disease – disease that they could pass to anyone.

This belief led to prostitutes being refused care or support, even in a medical setting. Elizabeth Stout was refused care at Lincoln Infirmary in 1841 on account of her being a prostitute and a thief. This story reached the *Stamford Mercury* and was reported by proprietor Richard Newcombe as a slander against Rev. Bagge. It stated that when she was delivered to the infirmary in a sedan chair in a very poorly state she was refused entry upon the rules of the infirmary that 'forbids admission into the house of those unfortunate wretches whose excesses have brought them to the gates of death'.[14] They stated that because there were no separate rooms, 'it would be a very monstrous thing indeed if the virtuous and good inmates of this asylum were to be contaminated by the example and intercourse with the most depraved of their species.' There was a long conversation about whether she should be admitted or not, with Rev. Bagge reminding the other gentlemen in the infirmary that the rules said she should not be admitted. With a lack of agreement, and despite Elizabeth being incredibly ill, she was sent away. The brothel she had come from refused to readmit her and she was forced to find a relative to stay with.

The story in the *Stamford Mercury* referred to Rev. Bagge as 'a cold-hearted moralist [who left] a poor fellow creature to perish for her sins'. Yet the court case proved that Rev. Bagge had followed Elizabeth and paid for a doctor and nurse to attend to her. He then visited regularly with his wife, ensuring she was well fed ('sago, arrow-root, chicken'), and in the hope that she would repent her life of sin. The jury believed the words of Rev. Bagge and the other gentlemen of the infirmary and found Newcombe guilty and liable for damages of £15 and 40s costs. Elizabeth was said to have inflammation of the peritoneum but there had been the suspicion that she had an infectious disease (venereal disease); all people with infectious diseases were to be barred as 'persons of this sort must always be suspected'.[15] Her undesirability excluded her from medical care, compassion and a house to rest in. The defence lawyer questioned whether it was acceptable to bar these women from all forms of support, and pointed out that she may well have died had she not been taken in by a relative. How many other women had died after failing to receive medical care because they weren't followed home by a god-fearing man?

How many women died because they were deemed to be already going to hell?

Harriet Ann Bottomley appeared in the *Leeds Times* in 1857 after claiming to have walked to Halifax from Liverpool while heavily pregnant. She had been born in Halifax but had lived in Liverpool for many years with her 'putative' father. After becoming pregnant she had been thrown out by her father and had gone to the guardians in Liverpool to request entrance to the workhouse for her confinement, as was the way with the poorest of women. They refused because she wasn't from Liverpool and her Liverpudlian father wasn't her 'real' father, and told her to go back to Halifax. Three times she asked for admittance, but all were denied, so 'without a halfpenny in her pocket'[16] she did as she was told and walked to Halifax, a distance of just under 60 miles.

The guardians in Halifax were horrified, claiming the Liverpool Guardians should have taken her in and charged them for keeping the girl. The Halifax Guardians took her in and made enquiries about charging Liverpool Guardians for their costs in a tit-for-tat exchange. There were concerns that if the Liverpool Guardians continued to send these women back that 'their streets would teem with prostitutes'.

Outspoken Women

Thankfully, there were a great number of outspoken and difficult women who were able to stand up for themselves or protest at their treatment. These included a great number of women who put up a fight or a protest at the point of arrest. Mary Ann Smith of Worcester is a great example of these women. Mary had been drinking with two men and was walking down the street singing with them at about 1 a.m. At the sight of the policeman, both men ran away, leaving drunken Mary to face the police alone. She was asked to 'go on quietly', but she didn't want to, so the constable attempted to arrested her; in protest, she laid down in the street.[17] He did manage to get her to the station and in front of a judge, who gave her a good telling off and sent her to gaol for a week.

Jane Bailey of Peterborough, another drunken prostitute, put up such a strong fight against her arrest that 'it took four constables to convey her to the station'.[18] She also received a week in gaol for her trouble. Similarly, Elizabeth Tilley was at Fortune's Well on the Isle of Portland in Dorset when she was accused of prostitution. Also drunk and rather violent, she had to be conveyed to the police station in a wheelbarrow for some of the journey![19] Phebe Ivett was arrested in the early hours in Huntingdon for 'being out in the streets at a late hour'.[20] She refused to walk to the gaol or say who she was, so she was taken in an omnibus (a horse-drawn bus) which was at least much more comfortable than a wheelbarrow.

Some women's voices come through in court cases where they are able to verbally spar with legal figures and stand up against wrongful treatment, convictions and penalties. Jane Marshall of Wisbech (see Chapter 1) was accused of stealing from John Cox while they were both in Stamford.[21] They had shared a room in the New Chequers Inn, which was run by Hugo Hickling, a landlord who ran his pubs as little more than brothels. After their encounter in one of the rooms of the New Chequers, John accused Jane of stealing his money, which she denied, skipping the town. She was caught and kept in gaol from her arrest in July until the Quarter Sessions in October. During her trial, in which she defended herself, she 'subjected the prosecutor to an unpleasant cross-examination and strongly protested her innocence', which led to her acquittal.[22]

The most famous case which appeared in every newspaper regarded Alice Millard (often written Maillard) in Aldershot, Hampshire in 1891. It should have been a simple case taken up with the magistrates. Alice had been arrested on the charge of being a disorderly prostitute. Police Constable Bradbury claimed she was a 'well-known prostitute', and '[h]e had seen her in the company of soldiers and talking to prostitutes'.[23] But Alice swore she wasn't a prostitute and was not prepared to have her name sullied by a policeman, saying: 'You cannot prove your words. Have you seen me with men in the pursuit of unlawful practices? I won't be charged with this offence.' Strong words from a 20-year-old woman in 1891. But the police doubled down, stating they were quite certain she was a prostitute and she was going to have to accept the charge.

In an unusual move they asked Alice if her mother was in court and then adjourned the case so that Alice could be taken to their family doctor by her mother for an examination. They returned with the doctor who took to the witness box. He said he had examined her and it was impossible that she was a prostitute. The case collapsed and the chairman reminded the police that they should be careful of who they accuse of being prostitutes.

This story was picked up by almost every paper in the country and was discussed in the House of Commons, being raised by four members of Parliament, one of whom suggested PC Bradbury should be tried for perjury.[24] The Home Secretary said he would look into it.[25] Indeed he did, and a perjury case followed for PC Bradbury and Police Sergeant Cottle. A vast array of witnesses were called on both sides but '[a]t least twelve of the witnesses called for the defence were of the most shameless and disgraceful character and their evidence was utterly undeserving of credit and untrustworthy'.[26] The judge asked the jury to ignore much of the evidence relating to the family and their poor conduct in Aldershot, not to be swayed by 'the friendliness' of Alice and to focus on the details relating to the case. The jury decided that Bradbury was not guilty and therefore neither was Cottle; the judge reminded the men that they should have made better enquiries as to her state before accusing her of being a prostitute.

The *York Herald* revealed information that other papers had not, in their summing up of the case in August. They stated that Alice's original arrest had come about as a result of trying to defend her mother while she was being arrested, and that Alice was drunk. She was 'kept in custody for three days and two nights, during which time the police endeavoured, without success, to make out a case against her'.[27] It seems that Alice's arrest and temporary incarceration had been brought about for attempting to help her mother. However, the reason Bradbury was not guilty of perjury was because he (and the other officers) all believed that she was a prostitute because of the company she kept, and her family. The paper went on to provide a moral note about Alice and other poor women: 'The conditions of her life are hard to begin with and are made harder by circumstances over which she has no control.' They claimed it was impossible for her to avoid the company of soldiers and 'loose people', and made it almost impossible to believe that she had kept her virtue. 'A little more sympathy, a little more belief in human nature, a little less selfishness and a little higher sense of the duty everyone owes to his neighbour, would soon produce a better state of things.'

A prostitute's reputation kept her from advancing in the world, from getting a fair hearing in trials and from accessing life-saving medical treatment. This is why women erroneously labelled as prostitutes fought to remove the damaging label, and why women who were no longer prostitutes did all they could to shake off their former status. It is also why these women were not afraid to resist arrest and defend themselves in court cases. With the label of 'prostitute' came an assumed immorality and therefore guilt for crimes that did not exist in other classes. Prostitutes were believed to be capable of infecting the population with both sexual diseases and immorality, and that made them dangerous. The view of a gentleman named 'Miles' from Bedford, commenting on the Contagious Diseases Acts, claimed that prostitutes chose to become prostitutes, which was a dangerous profession, 'as dangerous as if she stood at the corner of a street exploding gunpowder'.[28] Such comments only made the difficult lives of prostitutes even harder. It is at least satisfying to know that these comments were made in the light of people standing up for prostitutes and trying to repeal the acts. Having a reputation as a prostitute was a societal prison for some, for others it meant a continual fight to avoid prison. These women fought for their basic needs, for respect, for justice, but their reputation often barred them from anything but derision.

Life Stories: United in Death

It was not unusual for someone to die from the effects of fire in the Victorian era. The combination of long skirts, nightgowns, and open fires led to many tragic deaths, particularly for poor women and children who lived in small houses and couldn't afford a fire guard. Every house had a fireplace or hearth, candles and items such as gas lamps to light the rooms – open flames were a part of everyday life. However, these flames could also be used to destroy evidence of the most heinous crimes and occasionally the victims of them. Here we look at the deaths of three prostitutes who were all burned; one was a clear and deliberate act of murder, the other two were officially declared accidents…

The first death was in 1840, the second in 1844, and the third in 1863. They are unrelated, but there are parallels in men's violence, the misogyny of violent deaths, and of the lies and deception surrounding each case.

Jane Mackay

We start with the death of Jane Mackay. She lived on Union Row in the Barnwell area of Cambridge, which was described in the *Satirist* shortly before her death as 'the great eye-sore of Cambridge, the place where vice and dissipation reign supreme, where the tutor forgets his authority, the parson his cloth and the freshman his purity' (see page X for an example of the *Satirist*'s views on Barnwell).[29] Jane's death occurred in 1840, early in the Victorian era and before many towns were reporting issues with prostitutes. But this was a thriving university city; there was a healthy and continually changing population of young, rich, single men who had gained the sort of freedom they had been dreaming of for years. The university had been there for centuries, so there was a steady supply of young women and girls who were also discovering freedoms they had never known before and were trying to make a shilling or two in the slums.

At around 4 o'clock on the morning of 2 June, Jane Mackay was engulfed in flames. There were two conflicting series of events reported as to what happened. One version declared that she had been out drinking with a man, went back to her house and smoked a cigar before falling asleep on her sofa blind drunk, her accompanying gentleman helping himself to the bed upstairs. She woke, realised she was aflame and went upstairs to get her gentleman friend's assistance.[30] The other version claims that she had taken an undergraduate home and they went to bed upstairs. His cigar set light to the bedclothes and bed curtains and led to the destruction of several pieces of furniture, but he escaped without a scratch.[31]

In both cases her screams alerted the police who came to her assistance and put out the flames, barely saving the house from burning down. She could not be saved, however, and died three weeks later in Addenbrooke's Hospital (see page X for her death certificate). The ensuing inquest decided that she died an accidental death.[32]

It is the detail of this case that makes her death suspicious. The newspapers reported that the fire originated in different parts of the bedroom, her dressing table being 'reduced to ashes', yet she had supposedly slept downstairs on the sofa, which was undamaged.[33] The damage in the bedroom may give some weight to the idea that she ran about when she discovered she was on fire, but if Jane had slept downstairs, we have to ask why her instinct was to run upstairs to a sleeping man who would have had, at best, a pitcher of water to hand, rather than run outside to alert others or find the nearest pump. It's not completely implausible, given that a man was upstairs, but it's not entirely plausible either. We also have to believe that she was smoking a cigar and that she set light to the bed clothes and dressing table when she entered the bedroom on fire. Again, it's not impossible, but it sounds largely implausible, particularly given the total destruction of the dressing table. It's far more likely that she was in bed with the young man and one or both of them had been smoking.

Curiously, Jane provided a recount of the ordeal on her deathbed. She claimed that she was downstairs and set herself alight with her cigar. It was entirely her fault and no one else was to blame. Rather a strange thing to say on your deathbed in hospital, unless of course you'd been encouraged to make such a statement...

This takes us back to the man who was in her bed and to the rumours circulating about the incident that were alluded to in the *Cambridge Chronicle and Journal*.[34] The man was apparently an undergraduate; at the time, university was the reserve of the rich and powerful and that might be enough of a reason to wish to remove his name and any hint of foul play from his association with the event. However, the *Satirist,* claimed 'the Lothario found in Mackay's house was *not* an undergraduate but a *clergyman* and *Fellow of the University!*'[35] This would make her avowal that the fire was entirely her fault and she had slept downstairs all the more important. For a man of the cloth and university to be embroiled in such a scandal could leave him without friend, family, or career, but to create an element of doubt or push her admission of guilt to the forefront, would make his association all the weaker, should any witnesses claim he was the man in her house.

We have no description of Jane; we don't know how old she was, where she was from and there's no clue as to what she looked like. All we have is her deathbed confession that she had set herself alight smoking a cigar. We don't even have the first census to provide us with any information about her, which seems all the more tragic.

Hannah Bentley

The second story was either a tragic accident or a deliberate attempt to 'destroy' a prostitute. The woman was known as Hannah Bentley and she had been living at the Queen's Head in Elland, Yorkshire. In the early hours of a January morning in 1844, she was discovered alone 'in a collier's cabin, in Elland Park Wood, near Rawson's Arms Inn'.[36] She was horrendously burned, but taken to the Rawson's Arms where she was offered help before she died around 10 a.m. The Rawson's Arms Inn appears on Victorian maps (see page X) and sat on Elland Road by the Binns Bottom Colliery, so it would have been frequented by miners.[37] The inquest revealed that she had been drinking in the Rawson's Arms in the afternoon and suggested that she 'either crawled in the cabin or was persuaded to go there at night for shelter'. It was early January in Yorkshire and the inn was isolated in Elland Park Wood, so travelling back to Elland or beyond could have been a treacherous affair. Hannah was at the inn to make some money, so it's likely that when one of the miners suggested moving their evening to a little cabin nearby (which would have been free to use), she took him up on his offer. A collier's cabin was not designed for warmth or comfort, or indeed to last, but as a shelter from the worst weather at times when the colliers weren't in the pit.[38] It was likely, therefore, to have been rather cold.

The inquest stated she had been found lying 'opposite the fire and by some means her clothes were caught by the flames'. The description was deliberately vague because 'scarcely a vestige of clothing remained upon her person'. It was therefore impossible to know how her clothes caught light. It is possible that whoever went to the cabin with Hannah left her asleep after he had paid his dues, and a spark from the fire caught her dress alight. But let us remember an important fact: her death happened in a colliery building on colliery land with (almost certainly) a colliery employee. The colliery owners were going to ensure that whatever happened was cleared up as quickly as possible and any hint of something untoward would have been hushed up.

Trying to find the death certificate for Hannah proved impossible. However, a record did appear for the death of a *Martha* Bentley. According to a parish record, Martha was aged 26, was buried on 11 January 1844 in Elland, and was also the wife of James Bentley. Her death certificate confirmed that Martha died by 'accidental burning', and was the wife of James Bentley, a weaver, but it gives her age as 33 (see page X for her death certificate). Here we have a married prostitute, separated from her husband and making her way in the world by selling sex via local pubs using a different name. She would have known that every encounter she had with a man had the potential to end badly, but she would never have expected to have suffered such a torturous death alone in a collier's cabin.

This case serves as a reminder of the precariousness of prostitution and the risk that prostitutes working alone would have taken. We don't know if she accidentally set herself alight while alone in the cabin, or if she was the victim of foul play. Had she been with another woman, or in a room at the inn, her life might not have been extinguished in such awful circumstances. It is also another reminder of the difficulty of researching prostitutes because of their use of different names and wildly differing ages. However, whether she was 26 or 33, she was too young to die.

Betsy Brown

The third woman was Elizabeth Brown, aged 36, who was living in Whittlesey, Cambridgeshire, a small fenland town close to Peterborough. Her life was extinguished in the most violent of ways, so this case is not for the faint-hearted.

Elizabeth had met John Green, 'a fine, athletic young man of about 25 years of age', on 11 March 1863.[39] She was a known 'unfortunate', and lived next door to her parents in the town, where her father worked as a blacksmith.[40] The description of her in the paper was less than favourable, stating she liked to drink and smoke a long pipe and 'was a dark, coarse-looking woman', usually known as 'Betsy Brown'. Her friend Ann described her as 'a strong woman', and the *Lincolnshire Chronicle* added that she was tall and had 'high cheek bones and black hair'.[41]

On the night in question Betsy had been to a dance at the George and Star, now known as the George Hotel, in the Market Place in Whittlesey. There were many pubs in Whittlesey, but this was a large, prominent pub in a very public location overlooking the market, Buttercross, and St Mary's Church. Betsy and John had both been seen at the dance and left together when it ended in the early hours of 12 March. John was dressed in 'a white slop, cord trowsers [*sic*], a cap and a red neck-tie' (stereotypical 'country yokel' attire).[42] He was described as being 'rather tall, with dark hair and pale face, has no whiskers and is of slight but muscular build'.[43] They headed to Whyle's Maltings which were at the rear of the George and Star, and which was also John Green's workplace.[44] He had already stolen 'a bucket of gin from the George and Star', hidden it in the maltings with his friend and foreman George Smedley, and left the door to the kiln room open in case they wanted to return to it.[45]

John did return later to share the gin with Betsy. Despite having a wife and very young family at home, John had already 'gratified his unbridled lust upon her' before they reached the maltings, and he hoped to do so again that night, making use of the large settle.[46] But Betsy refused and a fight ensued as he attempted to have his way. In his own words from his later confession:

I pulled her off the settle. She kicked and knocked about and got hold of my hair and I tried and tried as long as I could to have connexion with her and when she would not, I hit her on the body with my fists and she fell on the floor. I then kicked her on the body more than once. She did not scream out. I then felt so bad that I did not know what to do, as I felt I had killed her. I stooped down and got hold of her and shook her and found that she was really dead. I then drank hearty of some more gin.

An opinion piece later suggested that if she hadn't put up a fight, 'she would in all probability have been alive [then]', which very much grates against twenty-first century values.[47]

When she was found, Betsy's tongue was protruding through her clenched teeth and her face was swollen. The doctors who examined her body (Dr Crisp from Whittlesey and Dr Clapham from Peterborough) found evidence that she had died of asphyxiation, something John did not allude to in his confession. They believed she had been killed by 'compression of the throat' by either 'the hand, arm, or knee' of her killer, which confirmed that her death was not accidental.[48]

John claimed he decided to dispose of her body by placing it in sacks and heaping 'a shovel full of hot cinders on the sacks', thereby lighting it.[49] The doctors identified several of Betsy's ribs and cartilage were missing, 'broken off by violence' according to Dr Crisp.[50] Also, part of her humerus (upper arm bone) was fractured and, so the doctors believed, had been cut 'by the introduction of an edged instrument' (e.g. a saw). It was missing from her body and only discovered some time later by George Smedley when he was sweeping the room.[51] Again, another strange event that has either been omitted by John or incorrectly identified by the surgeons.

In a rather gruesome confession, he admitted to watching her body burn for about an hour before he 'got up and drank some more gin and stirred up the burning sacks'.[52] He then fell asleep. When he woke, the room was filled with smoke and he was a little confused but found his way out and ran home. What he wouldn't have known in the confusion of the acrid smoke was that his attempts to destroy her body in the fire were not successful, destroying little more than her skirts and leaving her in a partly naked state with singed, cropped hair.

What he had not mentioned in his confession is that either he had removed the sacks, or they had burned through, for she was not referred to as being contained in any sacks. He had also arranged Betsy's body before he went back to sleep to look as though her clothes had caught alight while smoking, putting her pipe back between her teeth, despite her swollen tongue protruding from her clenched teeth. He also failed to recall stopping to defecate before his run home. John 'had a large evacuation of human faeces in a liquid state' on the street outside, some of which was still visible on his shirt later in the day, according to a policeman.[53] Dr Clapham explained that 'The sphincter muscle of the rectum is sometimes relaxed from a state of mental emotion', and knowing you could be hanged for the brutal murder of a prostitute might just do that to your sphincter muscle!

John ran home just before 6 a.m., being observed by several witnesses. He lived 370 yards away from the maltings so it didn't take him long to run home and see his family, possibly to ask his wife for an alibi, say goodbye to his three tiny children, or to wash some of the excrement from his body.[54] However, in his absence George Smedley had arrived at the maltings and in the gloom and thick smoke of the room thought he had stumbled across John's body. He ran out to get assistance, stating his fears in the street. One of the newspapers referred to the initial small-town panic of believing that it was John Green's body, his frantic mother wanting to know what terrible ordeal her son had suffered. But John appeared soon enough to allay his mother's fears, wearing a fresh cap. His other cap, the one he'd been wearing the night before, had been left at the crime scene, not far from the body. He was said to have smelt of smoke, not the smoke you might expect from a furnace, but he had 'an odour of burnt flesh about him'.[55] He also had singed hair, but it was agreed that it was impossible to know exactly when he had singed it.

The court case for John Green was exceptional in a few ways, predominantly because he was tried in December. Previously, the Cambridgeshire Assizes had been held in spring and summer, so this was the first time they had been held in the dark days of December. The reason for this related to another case in which a woman had been accused of a crime just after the summer assizes elsewhere in the country and had to wait until the spring assizes for a trial. She had been found not guilty and there were arguments made that the accused should not wait so long to discover their fate and be languishing in gaol in the meantime.[56]

The content of the case was also quite exceptional for the small, quiet town. The brutality of the case, added to the central location in the shadow of St Mary's Church (see page X for a map of Whittlesey), was also difficult for the local people to stomach. In addition, one of the key elements of the case was liquid excrement located in the street and on the clothes of the accused, further adding to the sensational nature of the trial.

The defence had little to persuade the jury that John Green was innocent of murdering Betsy Brown, other than attempting to discredit the views of the local surgeons, stating 'the whole case rested on the evidence of country practitioners, one of whom was a young man just commencing his professional career'.[57] The lack of motive for the murder was a factor that was pressed on the jury by the judge, but it made no difference.

The jury took only a quarter of an hour to decide John's fate: he was guilty. He had been locked in Chesterton Gaol in Cambridge and at 9 a.m. on 2 January 1864, he was taken to the scaffold and hanged. As one of the local papers stated: '*This* was a low and brutal murder, there was nothing of romance in it; and sickly sentimentality, for the nonce, could not be awakened even in the minds of those for whom the gallows has such repulsiveness.'[58] He was the last person ever hanged in Cambridge.[59]

These women suffered horrendous deaths. One was the deliberate brutal destruction of a woman, and the others were either drunken accidents, or also foul play. All three women lost their lives in an inhuman manner; all the stories remind us of the dangers of the life of a prostitute. Jane Mackay left nothing but her name and a confession that she had smoked a cigar; Hannah Bentley, little more than the knowledge that she was a married prostitute; and Betsy Brown left her name and a description of a tall, strong, pipe-smoking woman with black hair and high cheek bones.

These accounts are sensational, but that is not why they are included in the book. They have been included because they open a little door into a coal mining hamlet, a small provincial town and a large city. They provide insights into features of their lives, from the furniture in Jane's house, to Betsy's physical appearance and Hannah's choice not to walk home through a dark wood. Jane, Hannah and Betsy were at least provided with a decent burial, and they avoided the public and private scorn that the men who were involved were subjected to, but that's no consolation for three lives being snuffed out after spending the night with a man.

Chapter 4

Prostitute Haunts:
Where to Find a Victorian Prostitute

At every level of Victorian society, from dirtiest slums to the finest castles, women were selling sex. What separated the high-class and middle-class sex workers from the lowest, was power. Those women connected to powerful men lived in respectable houses and were slipping past the police and moralists by offending neither the eye nor the ear, and keeping their business behind closed doors. The greatest offence of lower-class prostitutes was to take their immoral practices into the shared spaces, blocking paths in the pursuit of a punter, befouling the air with their filthy language and dressing to impress with what little they had.

If we look back at the medieval period, prostitutes were often banned from towns and cities, including London, finding homes on streets outside of the thick stone walls or outside of specific areas, such as the infamous Southwark stews (stew was the medieval and Tudor term for a brothel) that were cited south of the Thames. Evidence of these views of marginalising prostitutes were still present in the Victorian period, for example, in Stamford, Lincolnshire. After complaints about a very visible pub-cum-brothel in the centre of town a comment was made that 'if such houses must be tolerated at all they should be allowed to exist only in the back streets in the outskirts of the town, removed as far out of the way as possible'.[1] Yet a brothel sited on the outskirts of the town, beyond the medieval walls, had been closed a short time before, and its keepers gaoled.

Housing

The majority of working- and criminal-class prostitutes could be found in the worst sort of housing. They didn't own their homes so, for those not living with their family, they rented a bed, a room, or a portion of a house (see page x for a rather sanitised version of how bad the housing situation was for some). That location might be rented for a single encounter above a pub, for a night's rest in a lodging house after an evening walking the streets, or on a longer basis in a brothel or home. Lodging houses were supposed to provide respectable housing for the poor, but were often associated with the immoral activities of prostitutes. New legislation was brought in during the era with the aim of removing their presence from the rooms of pubs, beerhouses and lodging houses (See Chapters 6 and 7), meaning that for much of the era prostitutes were more likely to be found in shared accommodation with other prostitutes. When the Castle beerhouse in Guildford closed in 1863, 'the women who had been kept there and others, had taken private houses near Mr Crooke's brewery' and were annoying their neighbours with their 'frightful disturbances at night'.[2] Without proof that these 'private residences' were being used as brothels and, more importantly, without complaints being followed through by these neighbours, there was nothing stopping the women continuing their noisy night-time activities because the police could not sanction their behaviour. Together, the women could earn enough to live in residences in a central location in the town, but on their own, they would almost certainly have had to live in small, undesirable housing such as slums.[3]

Slums were groups of poor-quality properties, built or owned by landowners hoping to make the most of their invested money. The properties were small, poorly lit, badly maintained and liable to damp, flooding and collapse. Built close together there was usually very little outdoor space and any they did have was communal, shared with their neighbours, their families, friends, pets and businesses. These homes were usually terribly situated, being infill at the back of pubs and inns, hidden behind dark passageways, or sited next to noisy and smelly industry, such as slaughterhouses, fish markets, or factories. In Lincoln, houses had been built in the infill of the castle ditch, known as Castle Dykings. Situated on the northern side of the castle walls the properties were obscured from the road and from any sunlight, making them dark and damp. But the location also provided the tenants with a veil of obscurity that benefited their activities: if they couldn't be seen, they couldn't be arrested.

There are clues on Victorian maps as to where slums and poor-quality housing were situated. From a lexical perspective, there are key words in the names of the streets and areas; yards, closes, alleys, 'back' streets and courts were all synonymous with poor housing. From a visual point of view, identifying small properties, often terraces and often square in shape, with little or no private outdoor space, or houses squeezed into locations where there shouldn't really be housing, are good clues that you've identified slums. Using examples from the Life Stories, Rosy Clarke's home in Peter's Court, Whitehaven, was squeezed in between Peter's Street, Charles Street and Queen Street; Catherine Thirkettle was in the overcrowded Rows area of Great Yarmouth; and Martha Baines lived in a tiny property on America Row in Leighton Buzzard. Another clue is if the properties have not survived the Victorian period and have been replaced by something else. When slum properties were removed, the area was often deemed unsuitable for further houses – and in prime locations it's surprisingly common to find them replaced by a carpark, offices, or shopping centres.

These slums were frequently owned by rich landlords – slumlords – who were looking to make a large profit on their residential investments with the least effort. In the Old Nichol in London, a vast area of slum housing, the landlords were rumoured to be 'peers of the realm, churchmen, Bethnal Green vestrymen and several corpses', which highlights both the lack of conscience, consciousness and regulation of the owners of the slums.[4] Slumlords around the country were vilified as houses fell into total disrepair and the very poorest of society died from the consequences of insanitary conditions and infectious diseases. This was the case in Angel Meadow, Manchester, where '[u]nscrupulous landlords stopped carrying out repairs and their occupants began using the houses' wooden frames as firewood, leaving them in a permanent state of ruin', as were the people who lived in them.[5]

Looking a little closer at the properties, we can discover some of the harsh realities of prostitute housing. Properties in Angel Meadow were in such poor condition that 'dozens of men and women [were] sleeping on the clay earth and broken flag floors', or were 'littered like human pigs upon shavings or chaff and almost without cover to their persons'.[6] In Seaham Harbour, County Durham, there had been a huge increase in prostitution in 1884 which led to the police raiding several premises known to be occupied by prostitutes. These were not brothels or lodging houses, but private shared accommodation. The conditions were dreadful and included seven women who lived together in one room in Back South Railway Street. In another house there were five prostitutes and seven children living in one room upstairs that measured 15ft by 12ft (4.5m by 3.6m). On the ground floor were 'four prostitutes, three children and two men regularly living'.[7] There was only one bedstead in the house.

Even if there was a bed, the women might have preferred the floor, given that many were filthy, damp and smelly. One lodging house in Huddersfield, Yorkshire, was described as being 'in the filthiest state possible', and 'the stench of the place was intoxicating'.[8] We might assume that only the most desperate of men would visit a prostitute in so disgusting a location, but the house was full of both men and prostitutes, one of whom was sleeping on a bed in a coal hole.

A brothel on Temperance Street in Torquay, Devon, was a particularly deplorable location. The house was run by William Bowden and Ann Waymouth, and was also home to their children: three little boys, a 12-year-old girl and a 19-year-old woman. There was only one mattress in the property, which was situated on the floor.[9] There were said to be clothes all over the place and a lot of nakedness – although it was the height of summer. There was a court case in 1890 when William and Ann were charged with running a brothel; at this time there were five prostitutes working in the house, one of them being William's eldest daughter. The couple were both sentenced to three months' hard labour after being unable to pay the £10 fine. The courts brought them up again in 1892 for keeping another brothel. Elizabeth Lemon was found lying on the floor and Jessie Jarvis was in bed with a man. It should be noted that the 1885 Criminal Law Amendment Act laid down harsher punishments for brothel keepers, as a stronger deterrent (see Chapter 7). In addition the 1889 Children's Charter had been created to protect children from the harm of living in brothels. It is therefore no surprise that when William and Ann reappeared, the youngest boys had been sent to Dr Barnardo's, and the younger girl to Mutley Industrial School in Plymouth. That left one child, Arthur, at home, and he was found in a disgusting state. Arthur was 10 years old and was 'covered in a mass of vermin marks'.[10] He was filthy, bruised, scarred and home to a personal colony of 'living vermin'. He was removed, his parents receiving four months of hard labour for running a brothel – and another month for neglecting Arthur. As awful as Arthur's condition sounded, consider that whatever vermin were living on Arthur also had a free run of the brothel and the women in it. Whether it was fleas, lice, bedbugs, rat bites, or a mixture of them, the prostitutes would not have been immune to the creatures and must have been covered in bites too.

Ann Hepworth's death at the age of 35 was certainly accelerated by her living conditions. Ann was not a well woman; she was an alcoholic and said to be 'diseased'. People had encouraged her to get help by taking herself to the local infirmary or the workhouse, but she refused to go. At the time of her death in 1845, she had been living in a hovel at the back of the Waggon pub in West Court, Sheffield. It had previously been split into two residences, with other prostitutes living on the top floor, but such was the poor state of repair that they had left. The building wasn't fit for habitation; the walls were constructed of laths and plaster, but the plaster had fallen off, leaving just the wooden laths which let the wind in. The roof was not sound, so rain penetrated into the room above and then down into Ann's room, removing the plaster on the ceiling, which had been replaced by sacking. The two tiny windows were largely defunct, the glass replaced by rags or not at all. To make matters worse, a form of cesspit sat against the side of the room, the smell entirely unhindered by walls or windows. Inside the hovel was 'an old broken bed on which she [Ann's body] lay; a broken chair and table'.[11] The police were initially unable to access the hovel, such was the smell, and the jury had difficulty viewing the room such was its diminutive size.

Ann was not alone in the room and shared it with a young prostitute named Matilda Osbourne, who paid for the room from the proceeds of prostitution. The judge at the inquest was incensed that properties like this were allowed to be lived in by humans, stating 'it was worse than a pig-stye'. A jury-member informed the coroner that it was one of a number of properties in so poor a condition, and that plenty of other people were profiting from renting rooms to prostitutes at above-market rates. Ann's death was ruled to have 'been accelerated by drunkenness and disease', with the judge stating that he would do all could to rid the area of such awful properties.

The circumstances of married women were not necessarily any better. Susan Cummings had been a notorious prostitute and short-lived brothel keeper in Stamford. At the time of her death, aged 67, she was living in a slum known as Spencer's Terrace and existed in almost unimaginable poverty. She died on the floor of her house, 'upon some rags' due to a lack of furniture.[12] At the inquest into her death, PC Lightfoot stated: 'There was not, to my knowledge, any bed in the house: the only furniture in the place were a small table and a chair with its back off.' The coroner decided it was her drunken temperament and a blow to the head that had caused her death, rather than her squalid home, but some furniture might at least have provided her with a dignified and comfortable end.

The Streets

Without the comfortable homes afforded to their higher-class brethren, working-class prostitutes regularly trawled the streets in search of their clients. There are many accounts of women blocking thoroughfares to accost passing men, with complaints made when it was too frequent, too lewd, or – heaven forbid – while congregations were leaving churches. The police reports provide a record of the streets most popular with prostitutes and these are largely the main routes in and out of towns, the roads closest to the most welcoming pubs, beerhouses etc., or the ones closest to where they lived.

There were known prostitute haunts where police would patrol the streets to move women on, or to launch a sting operation to catch a prostitute at work. These were carried out in order to clean the streets and make them feel safe for respectable men and women going about their business in busy thoroughfares. That's because the women were not afraid to launch themselves quite aggressively onto passing men in the hope that they could earn a little money. In an attempt to control their behaviour, some towns, such as Peterborough, gave warnings that prostitutes would be arrested if they were found in the streets after 10 p.m.[13] No such rules applied to the middle and upper classes, but prostitutes, women who were considered 'dangerous', were 'in need of regulation and containment'.[14] The regulation was designed to discourage and protect the prostitutes, but also to protect the other classes from theft, harassment and immoral scenes.

For those prostitutes without a brothel or lodgings, or who were carrying on their activities away from their family home, non-domestic buildings, beaches and fields, were often used for their activities. Hovels, stables, haylofts, outhouses and barns all featured in court cases involving prostitutes, particularly in more rural locations. We can assume they were hoping for a little privacy, a little respite from poor weather, or somewhere free to rest without having to spend what little money they had on a room.

Mary Allen, described by the press as 'a lady', travelled from Leicester to Loughborough for the Winter Fair in 1842, and met a man named James Hoyle, a drover.[15] With such a large number of people visiting Loughborough, lodging rooms would have been incredibly busy and it was also mid-November, so probably a little too cold to consider any alfresco sexual activities. The couple had met at the Waggon and Horses beerhouse and decided the privy was the best location for their connexion (a term often used in newspaper accounts for sex). This is far worse than it sounds, for it was during the Winter Fair when the town was filled with thousands of extra people – and long before flushing toilets. The smell of the privy must have been extraordinary, but it didn't seem to dampen James' lust. While James was distracted, Mary Allen stole 12s 6d from him, something he no doubt later regretted. Despite the shame of his unpleasant connexion, he wanted Mary Ann to face justice and he called the police. She was given six months' hard labour for the theft.[16]

Any location that a prostitute could sleep for free with protection, in the form of her willing client, was preferable to sleeping alone, be it a hovel, a field, or a barn. Lying next to a man was also a great time to rob him, particularly if he fell asleep. That is what Elizabeth Telford did after going into a field with William Casford just outside Whitehaven, Cumbria, on an August night in 1870. After visiting her room in a brothel, they went to a field just north of Whitehaven. While he slept, she stole a silver watch, watchguard and £1 5s, and appeared to flee from the town. She was caught in Penrith on 27 August and admitted to having the watch. Despite her admission and apology, she was sentenced to seven years' incarceration.[17]

Sleeping Outside

Sleeping outside was an offence under the Vagrancy Act, so any women found sleeping alfresco were arrested, regardless of whether they were prostitutes attempting to earn money or they were just incredibly poor.[18] Five hundred soldiers were billeted at the Weedon Barracks in Northamptonshire, and there were often accounts of women sleeping in the open air nearby. Jane Houghton and Ann Pettitt were among scores of women caught around the barracks. They were accused of sleeping in a rickyard (a yard for storing haystacks/ricks) and gaoled for three weeks for the crime. Another woman, Charlotte Groves, was given three months for sleeping in the open air.

It was the Cornish records that appeared to punish prostitutes for sleeping outside more than others. Elizabeth Ann Tremberth stood out the most for the horrendous cycle of poverty and (in the eyes of the law) criminality. Elizabeth was born in 1850 and lived in Redruth (the centre of prostitution in Cornwall). Elizabeth had been identified as a prostitute by her late teens, and by the age of 20 was classed as an old offender. In July 1870 she was sentenced to six weeks for sleeping in the open air. In the following year, after her fourth visit to prison, she was released on Saturday, 30 June. She was discovered sleeping on the quay at Truro by a policeman at 3 a.m. With no ability to support herself (and with four previous convictions) she was swiftly arrested and returned to gaol – less than twenty-four hours after she had been released. She received a month in gaol for that crime, being released at the beginning of August, but she was back in gaol by the end of the month after being riotous and disorderly. Gaol, in this case, was being used to keep Elizabeth off the streets – out of sight – punishments meted out not just for disorderly behaviour, but for being poor and homeless.

Affiliated Businesses

If a prostitute wasn't at home or on the streets looking for her next customer, she might have been found at a prostitute-friendly business, such as pawnbrokers, refreshment shops and public houses. Pubs were commonly associated with prostitution and landlords were frequently fined for allowing them to spend time on their premises.[19] The combination of alcohol and prostitution was a common bedfellow with theft, violence and public disorder, and it was thought that removing prostitutes from public houses would help to curb the trade. A vast number of prostitutes were identified in licensing cases under the Licensing Act of 1872 where local police delighted in running off lists of undesirable women who were seen, how often they were in the pub and how long they were there for. But some of the judges called into question the legislation, which stated a prostitute was allowed to enter a pub but not remain 'longer than [was] necessary to obtain reasonable refreshment'.[20] In theory, she could stay for a drink and leave, but the legislation was open to interpretation.

Sophia and Susan Bygrave, two sisters from Biggleswade, Bedfordshire, landed James Bentley of nearby Shefford a £3 fine after their behaviour in his pub in 1860 caught the eye of the local authority. After dancing with 'six strolling gymnastic performers' (which would have drawn a crowd, and therefore prostitutes), the sisters 'commenced singing obscene songs and exposing their persons'.[21] Businesses offering entertainment, particularly those which encouraged large crowds, were very popular with prostitutes. The more respectable would refuse entry to common or garden prostitutes but turn their eye to the respectable-looking variety.

Criminal prostitutes could be found at refreshment houses, theatres, concerts and dances, and as will be seen in the story of Susan Tingey, in music halls too. The Royal Casino, Concert and Dancing Room on Blundell Street in Liverpool was a common haunt for prostitutes in the late 1850s, as the Singing Rooms in Bolton had been in the previous decade. Letter-writing campaigns called on the immorality found in entertainment venues in big cities, leaving the behaviour of the smaller towns a little bit elusive. Indeed, the vast majority of the information relating to prostitutes and entertainment venues focuses on London and the multi-faceted array of fun on offer there.

The poorest, criminal prostitutes were often found in the most undesirable houses living in the most atrocious conditions. If they were unable to earn their keep where they slept, they were often discovered in the streets searching for their next payment. And when they were without a roof over their head, they were given one, in the form of the roof of the nearest gaol. Those that had a penny or two to spare would head to their nearest pub, beerhouse, or entertainment venue in the hope of enjoying themselves for a moment and possibly earning their next payment. They were at permanent risk of arrest for plying their trade on the streets, or being too poor to earn it, but they were at risk of illness, disease and potentially death if they stayed too long in their homes.

Chapter 5

A Rope of Sand: Friends, Foes and Families

Prostitutes did not live isolated lives, but were part of dense and complicated networks of people that included family, friends, brothel keepers, bullies and fancy men, policemen, beerhouse keepers, business owners and neighbours. The people present in the women's lives depended on their situation, location and for some, their temperament. Some women had employers who featured heavily in their lives, some had long-term clients, others had lodging-house keepers; those yoyoing in and out of gaol might have spent as much time in the company of police and magistrates as they did their own family and friends. For those who relied on the numbing effects of laudanum, their chemist might be an important figure; to those who spent more than they earned, their local pawnbroker might be equally as important. Alcohol was a necessary pillar of the lives of the majority of prostitutes, and the community of pub landlords, beer sellers and keepers of gin palaces, dram houses, taverns, spirit vaults, hotels and other drinking establishments, were vital for libations, as well as providing food, rooms, employment, opportunities to meet men, and a warm, dry alternative to their cold, damp homes.

Women

Successful prostitution relied on a network of women, primarily other prostitutes and brothel keepers. The *Stamford Mercury* described the connections between these women as being 'merely a rope of sand', after a high-profile prostitute was left in gaol awaiting trial, rather than being rescued by her friends.[1] The illusion was of strong, unbreakable connections, but the reality was that a woman in trouble could be immediately abandoned, the supposedly strong connections between the women gone in a gust of wind.

Brothel Keepers

The vast majority of brothel keepers were former prostitutes; it was career progression for older, tired, or business-savvy former prostitutes; or as the *Weekly Dispatch* claimed: 'females grown old in the path of depravity, in whose bosoms every spark of womanly tenderness had become quenched'.[2] They were female entrepreneurs, determined to make money from their pretty, drunk wards, and many were completely without scruples, offering up fresh meat at maximum profit to themselves and maximum harm to the women and girls they had coerced. Men were also identified as brothel keepers, but the business was largely a female endeavour and any men that were involved 'were rarely charged with keeping disorderly houses and seem to have enjoyed greater tolerance and lack of attention from the authorities'.[3] Many men who lived alongside their wives were punished for running brothels because they were the head of the household, but ultimately it was the women running the brothels, with the men often reminded by judges to keep their house in order.

Some brothel keepers continued to work as prostitutes while earning money from other women in their house, or they provided a home to prostitutes while raising a family, as Finnegan noted in York.[4] Some of these women ran beerhouses, pubs, or lodging houses, which provided a respectable front for their brothel; or they ran a discreet brothel in back rooms and upper floors, while their husband ran a legitimate business. Various legislation was introduced to curb the number of brothels hidden behind public and lodging houses, because it was largely impossible to hide these businesses – and drunken prostitutes rarely led quiet lives.

Fights between neighbouring brothel keepers were frequent. The cause of the quarrels were often left unstated in the papers, but punches were thrown, pokers were wielded and names called. Prostitutes were often embroiled in these fights, but they could just as easily be the victim of the brothel keeper's wrath, suffering beatings or other punishments including having their dresses taken. A prostitute's relationship with her brothel keeper was precarious, with the prostitute reliant on the roof over her head and/or the customers that frequented the house, yet also living at the whim of a keeper who only valued her for the money she made. The tempestuous and manipulative relationship between prostitutes and brothel keepers was one of the reasons, alongside legislation, that more women started living in shared houses of prostitutes (like Elizabeth Roberts), or with a 'bully' or 'fancy man' (see pages 69–70) as the era progressed. Living with other prostitutes provided a level support network for the women, which was infinitely preferable to the control of a brothel keeper, but prostitutes were just as likely to fight each other as brothel keepers were.

Prostitute to prostitute relationships are best represented as a friends and foes Venn diagram, with a considerable overlapping area. There were many stories of prostitutes falling out with their friends, and conversely falling out of pubs with their friends after drinking too much together. In newspaper accounts prostitutes were often found in pairs because they had gone out drinking together. They also worked together on the streets, acting as lookouts for the police, protectors and accomplices to thefts. There were a large number of prostitutes identified together in the streets accused of 'wandering abroad' together, being disorderly, or obstructing the footpath.

Maria Doody, Mary Ann Anderson and Elizabeth Leach were caught behaving 'drunk and riotous' in Wellington, Shropshire, in 1879, and epitomise the friend/foe relationship that prostitutes often had with each other. Mary Ann and Elizabeth were fighting in the street in the middle of the afternoon and 'making use of very foul language', which caused the local shopkeepers to complain because they were losing customers.[5] They parted, but the women's argument bubbled up again later in the afternoon, when Maria Doody went to Mary Ann's house and challenged her to a fight. They started exchanging blows in the street when Elizabeth appeared and stabbed Mary Ann three times: 'twice on the head and once on the arm'. The argument was because Mary Ann had previously lived with Elizabeth, but had left her to live with her friend Annie. The former friends had become mortal enemies and pulled their other friends into the affray. Elizabeth received six months for the attack.

Mothers

As Chapter 1 revealed, a woman's relationship with her mother could be the very reason that she became a prostitute. There were plenty of examples of prostitutes living and working in their mother's brothels, with the *Hull Advertiser* claiming it was 'a matter of fact that numbers of harlot-mothers train up their daughters in the same horrible vocation'.[6] But they could also be supportive, as Alice Millard's mother was, or good friends who went out drinking together.

Catherine Moore, known as Irish Kit, and her mother Ann were arrested in Churchgate, Leicester, in 1837 for being drunk and disorderly in the early hours of the morning. Ann, labelled as an 'ould woman', claimed she was arrested 'when she was quietly going for half-a-gallon of ale', and discharged.[7] Kit was labelled a disorderly prostitute and gaoled for fourteen days, highlighting yet again the difference in sentences handed out to prostitutes.

There were also mothers who were aware of their daughter's situation and had attempted to rescue them, such as Eliza Hill's mother in Heigham, Norwich. Eliza had been accused of stealing a coat and a sheet, and at her court case her mother claimed 'she had tried all she could to give her a comfortable home and reclaim her, but without effect'.[8] The Recorder therefore offered some compassion and only gave her twelve months' hard labour instead of penal servitude, her mother's words helping the situation.

Charlotte Eames' mother was brought into court at the Middlesex Sessions after her daughter (19) was accused of stealing four eggs. Charlotte worked as an ironer but was also known as a prostitute. Her mother claimed she 'had tried several times to get her into a reformatory, but [Charlotte] had begged herself off'.[9] Worse still, Charlotte was due to be married but her intended was horrified when he discovered that she was a thief; he knew she was a prostitute and 'thought she was going to reform', but theft was a step too far. Her mother's efforts of reform were in vain as Charlotte lost her fiancé and was gaoled for twelve months for her crime.

Men

The vast majority of the men who appear in the criminal cases were those of a very short term or fleeting association. Other men who appeared included those of a protective or supportive nature, such as family members, religious men and the police. Others included business owners, brothel keepers, husbands and romantic partners. These men represented every class and belief of man, from the poorest to the upper classes, and from the biggest sinners to the most devout. As Kellow Chesney succinctly stated in *The Victorian Underworld*: 'Nothing formed so close a bond between the underworld and respectable society as prostitution.'[10]

Fleeting Associations

What is very obvious from the newspaper reports is that clients of prostitutes were largely local working men representative of the largest employment. In rural areas (or centres of an agrarian economy e.g. market towns) they were agricultural labourers and farmers who had gone to town to sell their goods and spend the proceeds on a little fun before returning home; in coastal areas they were sailors, smacksmen, watermen, coastguards, and even sand artists; in mining communities: colliers, excavators and miners; in university cities (Oxford and Cambridge): undergraduates and academics. These were not a particularly niche demographic of depraved men, they were ordinary men. They were single and married, young and old, rich and poor.

The occupations of the men engaging with prostitutes represented not only the major employment opportunities, but also the changing prosperity and industry of areas and the country as a whole. As new jobs were created by industry and invention, so they were reflected in the men found with prostitutes. Railway labourers appeared where the railways expanded, excavators where the underground was being built in London, navvies when engineering projects were underway, and factory workers when new factories were built. The men who worked there were often away from their families, or were young single men who were looking for a little fun.

Some men had jobs that were at the cutting edge of new technology, such as photographer James Haywood for example, who had been the victim of a theft by Ann Haddell in 1863 in Worcester, and was also arrested in 1864 with Mary Ann Thomas for being drunk and disorderly.[11] Others were men of once common but now obsolete or niche occupations, such as furnaceman George Bartley who was robbed of 'a sovereign and half crown' by Matilda Simpson in Dudley; ostler John Barwell who had his purse stolen by Caroline Meager in Penge; and chimney sweep William Dawson who was caught having sex with Martha Gough on Fairfield Path, Croydon.[12]

Respectable Men

As well as the more common farmers, navvies and general labourers, prostitutes were also visited by men of a more respectable nature – those of the middle classes. George Hinchcliffe, a wire card manufacturer (another obsolete occupation), complained he was the victim of highway robbery by three prostitutes at Frome, Somerset, in 1875.[13] George was on his way home from a dinner with the Ancient Order of Foresters (a respectable friendly society) when he claimed he was accosted by Sarah Clarke (17), Julia Ransome (18) and Louisa Clarke (28). Together they stole money worth £13, and £40 worth of rings (three diamond and one onyx), and then hid the items around their house on Butts Lane, where it was later discovered by an eagle-eyed policeman.[14] The women were accused of highway robbery, which came with a severe penalty. George was keen to withdraw the case, partly because the women claimed he gave them the money and rings as payment 'for an immoral purpose', but the case went ahead. He claimed that the women had 'jostled against him' on his way home from the George Hotel, but the women claimed he'd been drunk on champagne and quite insistent to make their acquaintance.[15] Two of them went with him to his premises (his Wire Card Works on Christchurch Street East), where acts unfit for publication took place and he handed them money and rings in payment. When the case reached the Somerset Quarter Sessions the women were unrepresented and struggled to defend themselves. Their claims of 'unpublishable acts' were said to have been impossible in the fifteen-minute window after George left the hotel and arrived at the police station. The judge was unsympathetic to the women's explanation and guided the jury to find them guilty, but their impassioned speech had the desired effect and all three were found not guilty. Perhaps they had considered how difficult it would be to remove four rings from a man's hands after a 'jostling' in the street and found him an entirely unreliable witness…

Upper-Class Men

Where there was an overwhelming stigma to being a prostitute, it was not the case for men engaging with one (unless they were of the highest moral standards). Prostitutes, it was believed, met the needs of men in society; they were a specific, separate class of women demarcated for a specific purpose. This was something that upper-class men knew as well as the lower classes. For the upper classes it was accepted that a man could take a mistress (there are some famous royal mistresses) and mete out his sexual proclivities as he wished, as long as these were as discreet as possible, to avoid bringing shame to his family and society (see page X for an artist's impression of some of these behaviours).

In December 1866, the *Cheltenham Mercury* broke the story that a ball had taken place at the York Rooms, Cheltenham, that was nothing short of an orgy.[16] The paper had received an invitation to the ball on 6 December from Miss Alice Williams which was 'under the auspices of a Captain Henry, holding the Queen's Commission, and protected by members of the County Police Force.' The paper claimed the ball was 'nothing better than an encouragement to harlotry', and were incensed that such debauched behaviour could occur in their town. They demanded an inquiry as to how such a ball could take place and how it could be organised by a respected captain.

The event quickly became known as the 'Prostitutes Ball' and it frothed up the sensibilities of the locals. Captain Henry had asked Alice Williams to be the hostess of his ball, at which '"a large number of women of abandoned character" with their "protectors", were invited as guests.'[17] They dressed in 'fancy and evening costume' and dined on oysters and champagne. It was also believed that Captain Henry had been supported by a school master and a professor of music. A *Cheltenham Examiner* article emphasised the point that neither the police nor the magistrates could have put a stop to the event because it was held in private behind closed doors and therefore no crime was committed. It was down to public pressure to bring the organisers to account for their immoral behaviour.

The *Mercury* continued to reveal details of the ongoing story, despite Captain Henry's denial that he was engaged in such immoral practices. They were also not deterred when the newspaper's office was surrounded by Alice Williams and her friends in an act of intimidation.[18] One thing the paper did do was name him fully as Captain Charles John Henry. Census records show that he was born in Ireland and was 60 years old at the time of the ball. He lived in a large villa in Cheltenham with his wife, Lady Selina, three daughters and seven servants.

Other newspapers indulged in the scandal, taking veiled swipes at Captain Henry for reducing the morals of the upper classes to those of the lower. The *Bristol Times* stated that Alice Williams was the mistress of another (married) man at the Imperial Club in Cheltenham, and it was through connections at the club that the participants of the ball were sourced.[19] Once the scandal developed, members attempted to ban him from the club, but they didn't have enough votes to enact it. In fact, he stayed in Cheltenham, ignoring all of the vitriol directed towards him.

What makes the situation far worse was the position of the Captain's wife, Lady Selina Constance Henry. A few months earlier, in February 1866, she had held her own ball and invited the very best of society.[20] It was an 'elite' event, with many of the honourable guests named in the paper to highlight the respectability and patronage of the event. When her husband held a ball filled with prostitutes and his friends from the Imperial Club, he was undoubtedly mocking the society she kept – whether she was aware of the ball or not. The delivery of the invitation to the *Mercury* may suggest that Captain Henry expressly intended to embarrass his wife with maximum effect, and used the prostitutes as pawns in his game to humiliate his wife.

Less than a year later Lady Selina, daughter of the Marquis of Hastings, died, aged 57, leaving behind three grown up daughters and her morally bankrupt husband. There is a portrait of her in the National Galleries.[21] Her face is one consumed with regret and her shoulders seem to bear the weight of the world; a regretful reminder that for every prostitute-visiting husband, there was a wife sitting at home.

Other upper-class men enjoying the company of prostitutes at the cost of their family's reputation include Lord Marcus Beresford, brother of the Marquis of Waterford, who enjoyed 'distinguishing himself in the streets of York in the company of prostitutes' in 1870.[22] This was by no means the last time his name entered the papers in a scandal! And if you haven't read the case study of The Tingey Sisters yet, look out for Sir Joseph Capel Judkin-Fitzgerald and the downfall of his family name.

Religious Men

The ultimate coup for a prostitute was to entangle a religious man, the very men who damned immoral women from the pulpit and led their congregations from positions of moral superiority. One of the most interesting stories involved a rural vicar and an affair across two countries.

Herbert Charles Marsh was vicar of the idyllic village of Barnack, near Peterborough, and the son of the Bishop of Peterborough, Herbert Marsh. He had taken up his position in the village in 1832 at the age of only 24, after it had been vacated by Charles Kingsley. Sadly, he developed a taste for French prostitutes and, in 1839, discovered Nathalie Miard, a French prostitute; he visited her in both England and France.[23] Their connection lasted several years because Nathalie was shrewd; she knew that she had her own infatuated cash cow, and milked him for every penny she could. She claimed to give birth to his child (and therefore his heir) and demanded money to pay for the costs of raising it. She asked for increasingly greater sums of money even after the supposed child had died, and was quite incensed when he started to ignore her demands.

Nathalie lived in both Paris and London during the time that they were acquainted, which was plenty of distance for the vicar. However, after providing her with hundreds of pounds over the next few years, he started to refuse her demands. In the spring of 1843 she arrived in nearby Stamford, taking a room at Standwell's Hotel, and threatened him again. The letter she sent him stated her plan:

Firstly, I will go to your church on Easter-day and reckoning from that evening, I will go into your village, from cottage to cottage, to inform them all of that which has passed. Afterwards I will go to the Magistrates at Stamford and from Clergyman to Clergyman at Peterboro', to all the Chapters and to the Bishop. I will take afterwards the names of all the Bishops of England and I will write to them all. From there I will go to London and cause you to be published in all the newspapers. Afterwards I will go to find the Archbishop of Canterbury, who shall be equally instructed; and I will go again to London to the Magistrate.

She was good to her word and arrived in Barnack at Easter, where she attempted to fluster Herbert in church, but he had absented himself. Over the next six months she was able to embarrass him in by entering the church during services 'in the most marked manner, and invariably arrest[ing] the attention of the congregation'. She also contacted several important people including his mother and attempted to extort money from his brother, George.

This was the final straw and his brother went to the police. The ensuing court case caused an enormous scandal locally, but also nationally due to the vast sums Herbert had sent to Nathalie, the growth in popularity of non-conformist churches and subsequent dissenting views about the wealth and control enjoyed by the Church of England.

Despite a considerable amount of evidence to suggest that Nathalie had attempted to extort a large quantity of money from Herbert and George, the jury agreed that she should face no charges, but be returned to her native country. This was, it was claimed, due to several dissenters sitting on the jury.[24]

John William Johnson of Canonbury, London, 'who described himself as a clergyman', was arrested for being drunk and disorderly with Eleanor Brandon, a prostitute.[25] They'd been out drinking together in Islington and were a little beyond tipsy. When a policeman found them they were fighting each other in the street 'one with an umbrella and the other with a stick.' The cause of their drunkenness was apparently the sherry they had imbibed at John's house after he had invited her in. They both paid a fine of 10s and promised not to do it again.

Rev. John Jones was the vicar of Cradley, a village in Dudley, West Midlands. He was a married man and, in 1843, was accused of striking up a familiarity with a prostitute named Mary Ann James who lived in a brothel in Birmingham.[26] He travelled to Birmingham to see her several times and even took Mary on two-day trips to Stratford and Lichfield in the summer. He'd also written her letters, using the pseudonym 'George Hallen'; Rev. Jones' handwriting matched that of the letters. He didn't find himself in front of his local magistrates, but under the eye of neighbouring clergy, who, after a thorough investigation, found him guilty of adultery. He then 'received an inhibition from the Lord Bishop, to prevent his performing the duties of the church'.

The story did not stop there, however. Although the original case had reached the papers in 1843, it was still being discussed in the following year. Rev. Jones was determined to clear his name and prove a case of mistaken identity. However, the evidence against him increased when a witness for the case against him claimed he had been to visit Mary Ann James in the brothel 'as many as ten times'.[27] After several days of deliberation the evidence against him was found conclusive and he was 'suspended from his office for two years'.[28]

This case in the Arches' Court followed that of Herbert Charles Marsh and preceded the case of Rev. Arthur Loftus of Fincham St Martin, Norfolk. He had been accused of 'intercourse with prostitutes, frequenting houses of bad fame, obtaining his domestic servants from a notorious procuress and sharing them with his footman'.[29] He was found guilty of the crimes, but his defence of his profligate ways were 'that his debaucheries had been pursuant to medical advice' – his doctor told him to do it! Was this because he had a nasty case of syphilis and his doctor believed that sleeping with a virgin would cure him of the condition? (A common belief, and one of the reasons virgins commanded such a high price.) Or was he clutching at straws? Either way, he was banned from preaching for three years.

The vast majority of associations between religious men and prostitutes were those of protection and redemption. Penitent homes were always supported by local religious stalwarts and time and again it was religious men who offered to help remove young women from places of harm and help them to find a new life. One or two visible warts should not sully the face of overwhelming positive religious endeavours.

Long Term Relationships

These are the men who usually appear the least in the newspaper records with prostitutes. It is usually through census records, death records and inquests that they are discovered, although men of a particular violent nature also crop up.

Prostitutes are, by the nature of their work, often without a partner or husband while earning their income through sex work. Marrying and cohabiting often removed a woman from the trade, despite her still being labelled so by the police. The cases of violent men such as Charles Savage, who knew his partner Jane Holland was working as a prostitute in Crewkerne but attacked and killed her for flirting with another man (see pages 143–4), were less common than the papers might like us to believe, but violence and abuse was commonplace.[30]

More common were examples of partners living off the women's illicit income. Ellen Swaysland was attacked by William Edmunds in Brighton in 1860. They had been living together off her prostitution for about six years, but she had been struggling to earn any money due to the poor weather. Ellen stated to the magistrates: '[w]hen he came home this morning he gave me a black eye and took up the knife produced and threatened my life'.[31] He had beaten her many times, as the bruises on her body testified. William was lectured by the magistrate 'on the brutallity [sic] of his conduct', and sent to gaol for three months.

Jane Emery had been living with George Lynn in Brighton in 1860. He also lived off her prostitution and had been doing so for the previous three years – Jane was 16. In court she 'scarcely ceased crying during the time she was detailing her evidence', as she explained how he had 'kicked her three or four times in the stomach' in the street.[32] Her beatings were frequent and he had caused a pregnancy to end in a still birth a year earlier. George was gaoled for three months for his mistreatment of Jane.

George Anthony Temple was living off the income of Alice Campbell in Newcastle when he hit her in 1899. George wasn't working, relying instead on money that Alice gave him, but it wasn't enough for him. He pawned her clothes and when she had no more money to give him 'he struck her – on the mouth and in the eye'.[33] Thankfully, the laws had changed by the end of the century (see Chapter 7) and George was sentenced to one month for hitting Alice and another two months for living off her trade.

Fathers
Fathers occasionally appear in the records, notably when a young prostitute wishes to return to her family but her father rejects her. The father of Elizabeth Watson Howe was contacted after she had attempted to end

her life in Norwich at the Foundry Bridge, by the train station, in 1861. He was a parish clerk living in Walsoken, Norfolk, at the time, and sent a letter in response stating: 'I cannot think of taking my daughter home again. I have done so several times but to no avail.'[34] He did ask another clergyman to visit her in the hope she was finally penitent, but made it clear that he would not 'disturb the peace of [his] home again'.

Just as mothers were accused of causing a woman to enter into prostitution, there were also fathers accused of the same. William Taylor appeared before the magistrates in North Shields in 1891 for assaulting his daughter, Hannah, after she dared to sit on the quay with her sister. He was furious because he was a fisherman and worked at the quay, and the sight of Hannah, who worked as a prostitute, 'degraded him in the eyes of his employers'.[35] He had beaten Hannah many times before though, so this was not a one-off event. When asked if she relied on the support of her father she replied: 'I'm only an unfortunate, but my father drove me to it.' He received a fine of 10s and costs.

Supportive or Protective Men

The word supportive is loosely used here and can refer to a man protecting the prostitute from harm, to ensuring she has everything that she needs, spiritual or friendly support or advice. Support was offered through the workhouse and charities, penitent homes and gaol time. Many of the magistrates were happy to incarcerate women in the belief that time away from their immoral lives would let them see the error of their ways and turn them away from licentiousness. Likewise, the work of police to remove drunken women to gaol in wheelbarrows and carts was to protect them from harming themselves and other people. Identifying and arresting the perpetrators of assaults and violence against women also helped to protect the women.

In an unusual case in Winslow, Buckinghamshire, in 1853, Bridget Power's husband, John, came to her defence after she stole the contents of a purse whilst having 'improper intercourse' with Henrey [sic] Linney, a father of six.[36] He 'forcibly addressed the jury on behalf of the prisoner and in strong terms denounced the conduct of the prosecutor,' seemingly able to ignore the fact that his wife was also having 'improper intercourse' outside of marriage. His plea was, however, successful and she was found not guilty. Despite appearing to allow or encourage his wife in immoral behaviour, he was at least prepared to defend her.

A prostitute plying her trade on the dark streets of a town or city was at risk of harm, from other women, from men who would rather resort to violence than pay their way, and from unscrupulous brothel keepers. Something a prostitute could do was to find herself a 'bully', or protective figure. That might be within a brothel, where the bully protected all of the women in the house, or individually, often with a personal relationship with the man.

The men closest to the prostitutes were termed 'pals', 'fancy-men', 'bullies' and 'companions', but the term 'pimp' was not used in the newspapers. In Hanley, Staffordshire, in 1845, George Wilkinson was labelled as a 'bully' and sent to gaol for two months for violently attacking Mary Johnson, a prostitute under his supposed protection. He had attacked her because she had gone to the police after being assaulted by another man, which broke 'the understood rules of the community'.[37] The word 'bully' might have been new to the paper, but the rules of the community were already well established by the early years of the Victorian era.

At the meeting of the town council in Bolton in 1842, there was the suggestion that the night police should be removed from the town to save some money.[38] However, it was claimed there were 'some hundred and fifty prostitutes prowling about the streets and to support these … at least, one-half the number of prostitute bullies'. This suggests that the women were living alone or in small groups, and potentially that the level of violence or fear of arrest in Bolton was significantly high enough to warrant individual protection for each woman.

This was certainly the case for Emma Twidall, who suffered a brutal beating in her brothel in Hull in 1862.[39] Charles Thompson went back to Emma's room with her and realised he didn't have any money to pay her. He offered her his undercoat and coat until he could return with change, but she refused him. In a rage he attacked her with a shovel, 'rendering her insensible' and confined to bed. He claimed to have 'used the shovel in self-defence and to save himself from the expected attack of a "bully"'. Following an earlier felony conviction, he received eight years in gaol.[40]

Fancy men were there to support the prostitutes as friends or lovers. They were the men who sold on stolen goods, or who received items that had been pick-pocketed in pubs and brothels. A fancy man named Wooler was connected to the hocussing (drugging to knock someone out) of a druggist in Leeds in 1846. Ann Carr (22) and Mary Daley (22) had been drinking gin with Zachariah Senior, who was visiting Leeds from Bradford and filling time before his train arrived.[41] As he walked to the station he collapsed in the street and came around in the station house where he'd been rescued. His 'gold watch, gold pendant, a brandy flask, case of surgical instruments, cigar case, silk handkerchief and gloves' had been stolen. Wooler was identified after attempting to sell the gold watch for £16 to a silversmith. He was referred to as a 'pal' or 'fancy man' of the two women. He received one week in gaol for his involvement; Mary received a year, and Ann six months.

Fancy men were commonly involved in theft cases with their prostitute companions, as was the case with Sarah Ann Firth, Winnifred Brotherwick and their fancy man George Broadbent in Halifax in 1854. They were accused of 'robbing a flat [someone easily deceived], named William Iliffe, of £5 10s, at Andrew Dearnelly's beerhouse', but were let off when William failed to show, hoping to avoid an 'exposé'.[42]

The people involved in the lives of Victorian prostitutes served a variety of roles, some supportive and some aggressive or exploitative. Women's relationships fell largely into the friend/foe type, whereas men's relationships varied based on what they wanted from, or could give to, the woman. The connections of prostitutes reflected society, both regionally and nationally, based on changing employment opportunities and even the position of the church. Elsewhere in the book are examples of the rise of female empowerment and women fighting back against misogynistic oppression, but also the women who discovered kind husbands or were offered escape from dangerous situations by religious men. For many, their relationships were difficult, but they weren't all bad.

Life Story: Martha Baines

Martha Baines was born in Leighton Buzzard in 1846 to Richard and Eliza Baines. Richard was a labourer, working first on the land and then on the railway. Eliza was a straw plaiter, as were a large number of the women in Bedfordshire and neighbouring counties. The industry was an integral part of the area and paid reasonably well, particularly for the local women. But it was also a very time-consuming cottage industry in which 'deft fingers often plied long into the night making hundreds of yards' of plait, such was the demand and desire to earn money.[43]

In the 1861 census, Martha's father was labouring on the railway and one of her brothers was working in a brickyard, but Martha, her mother and four other siblings – the youngest only 7 – were plaiting. The work required nimble fingers but no formal education, meaning that rates of literacy were low in the plaiting districts.

In the same year, Martha, aged 15, was accused of stealing 'a quartern loaf' of bread from Catherine Pratt's shop.[44] The magistrates decided she had probably stolen the loaf at the request of her parents and therefore sentenced her to three months in Bedford Gaol to teach them all a lesson. Rather than scaring Martha straight, it seems to have had the opposite effect by introducing her to more hardened criminals. It was at that point that she went from a small-time criminal to a town nuisance.

Her second visit to Bedford Gaol was on 1 July 1864 when Martha was 17 or 18.[45] Accused of damaging a rose tree, she was described in the *Leighton Buzzard Observer* as a 'young woman of ill fame', in the *Bedfordshire Times and Independent* as 'a troublesome prostitute', in the *Bucks Advertiser and Aylesbury News* as 'one of the "frail sisterhood"', and in the *Bedfordshire Mercury* simply as 'a prostitute'.[46] Alfred Giles was a shoemaker in the town and had a rose tree in his front garden, behind a fence. Martha was said to have reached over the fence to break the rose tree and then pull it up from the roots. When he went over to remonstrate with her, she said 'if he said anything further about it, she would smother him in the dunghill'. When he went to get a summons she assaulted him, giving him a bloody nose and a cut mouth, meaning he was covered in blood when he arrived in front of the local magistrate Major Hanmer.

She failed to turn up for the hearing and was sentenced to twenty-one days' imprisonment in her absence.

In the following October Martha was in Ledburn, a hamlet southwest of Leighton Buzzard. She had been at a statute fair at the Hare and Hound pub and was walking home behind a policeman, PC Clark, when he came across two men named Joseph Cook and Thomas Arnold. Joseph and Thomas had taken 'three tame fowls' from the pub grounds and were discovered by PC Clark hiding under a hedge. He immediately thought they looked suspicious and noticed something large in Thomas Arnold's pocket as he approached them.[47] As he tried to find out what they'd got, a scuffle broke out at which point PC Clark grabbed Thomas but was pinned to the floor. Martha, who hadn't been part of the fowl theft, couldn't resist getting involved and pulled PC Clark's hair and joined in the assault to try to release Thomas before the three of them ran off.[48] Three dead fowls were found later, close to where the men had been hiding. They were all arrested and hauled up in front of the Quarter Sessions. The jury sentenced the two men to three months in gaol, but acquitted Martha.[49]

In 1866 she was discovered drinking in the taproom of a beerhouse run by John Cosby with her friend Ann Stevens.[50] Both were labelled as common prostitutes which meant Cosby had committed a crime by allowing them to drink there. He was fined 5s with 14s 6d costs. Only a month before, the two friends had been sent to gaol for 'fighting and behaving in a riotous and indecent manner'.[51] Martha received fourteen days and Ann seven.

Martha had not been welcome at John Cosby's beerhouse since his fine, but when, in 1869, he went out for the afternoon and left his daughter in charge, Martha turned up. Martha was told to leave by his daughter, but she was abusive and refused. When the police were doing their rounds in the middle of the afternoon she was dancing to a fiddler, but when they returned later in the day she spotted them coming and fled, fearful she would be arrested. Cosby was fined, again – Martha escaped.[52] Like many prostitutes, she had so far been associated with thieves and other prostitutes and found in or near drinking establishments. Martha's personality peeks through the records in positive and negative light; we know she liked to dance to a fiddle, but we also know she could be vindictive and threatening.

In July 1870 she appeared in court on two separate charges. The first was for assaulting a woman who spoke against a friend in their court case, for which she was fined. In the second she was convicted of obstructing the police in the execution of their duty with three other people.[53] They had encouraged two men who were being arrested to resist against their arrests (just as she had with Thomas Arnold). The court was not impressed and rather fed up of seeing her, so she was given a month in prison in lieu of a fine.

In 1868 Martha, aged 22, had a child, a daughter, named Emma after her sister. Two years later, at the very end of 1870, she had a second daughter, Ann, meaning she'd been noticeably pregnant while incarcerated. Captured in the 1871 census, her small family were living together in Mill Road, a few doors down from her parents (see map on page X). Martha was unmarried, which by Victorian standards made her children bastards and her a prostitute, but this was surprisingly common among plaiting communities. The wages supplied by plaiting allowed women to support themselves; they could afford to live alone and away from the control of their parents or a husband. Without that control they were afforded sexual and financial freedoms unavailable in other parts of the country, or as some local employers who struggled to find workers claimed, it made them a little 'saucy'![54] This state of independence was something that female workers could only dream of in other parts of the country.

A year later in 1872 Martha found herself in court accused of assaulting her neighbour Sarah Brandom. At the heart of the argument was the accusation that Sarah had 'taunted her with regard to the circumstances of the death of her illegitimate child'.[55] Thomas Baines – her first child – had been born in 1866, when Martha was only 20, and had died a few months later. At the inquest of his death Martha revealed that she had got home to her lodging at about 2 a.m. and found Thomas asleep.[56] He woke at about 7 a.m. and they both went back to sleep, but when Martha woke a couple of hours later, she discovered Thomas stiff and black in the face, something her landlady corroborated. The doctor decided that Thomas 'had died from suffocation through having been overlaid by [his] mother'. Martha had killed Thomas, but crucially she had not intended to and it was a very tragic accident, something that still hurt deeply six years later.

Martha was clearly traumatised by the child's death and took it upon herself to get revenge on the woman who suggested she had caused his demise. She had taken the child's death certificate with her to prove to the magistrates that she had not killed her child and that she was quite correct to assault her neighbour for slander.

Martha was said to have followed Sarah's daughter Mary Ann home and, after arguing, crashed through her front door with her before lunging at Sarah and pulling chunks of her hair from her head. Martha's sister Emma had also got involved in the affray, attacking another neighbour who was there at the time and tearing off her 'bonnet and hair net'. Emma later revealed that she was quite annoyed that her 'three-and-sixpenny feather' had been lost in the affray.

Both sisters were convicted of assault. Martha was fined 5s with 9s costs and Emma 5s with 7s costs. Martha claimed she could not pay and Emma said she would not pay, so they both went to prison for fourteen days. We must presume that Martha's children went to stay with her mother.

In 1873 she was labelled a 'North End Vixen', in reference to the street she was on, after a squabble with fellow prostitute Mary Pratt.[57] The argument started with Mary fetching two pails of water from the well and another woman – Mrs Cotching – who 'fouled the water she carried in one pail'. A fight began between the women and Martha waded in, having had a long-standing feud with Mary. Water and punches were thrown, hair was pulled and kicks landed. The magistrates dismissed the case due to all the contradicting evidence, forcing the women pay their own costs as a punishment. Martha, it seemed, enjoyed a good fight and didn't need much of an excuse to join in.

The following year Martha was fined for not sending her children to school. By this point Emma would have been 6 years old, and Ann 4. Martha was one of four families fined for not sending their children to school and she, along with a man named William Bates, showed 'a considerable amount of temper and stubborn disinclination to obey the law'.[58] Both parents were used as an example for other neglectful parents and were charged under the Workshops Regulation Act of 1867.[59] It is likely they were made an example of in anticipation of the Agricultural Children Act (1873), which banned children under 8 from working, meaning Martha's children would have to attend school.[60] The fines were designed to act as a warning to other parents to encourage their children to attend school, but the Act is now viewed as terribly ineffective; the fines to parents were so small that they were financially better off by letting their children work and paying the fine from their salary, than going without their salary altogether. In an area where straw plaiting was embedded into the culture, and an industry that offered a reasonable income and opportunities for even the smallest of fingers, the prospect of a fine was no deterrent at all.[61]

In 1876 Martha became embroiled in an inquest involving the death of Mary Ann Favell. Mary Ann, known as Polly, lived at home with her mother and four brothers, and next door to her brother Elijah, who was married to Martha's sister Emma.[62] When the family rose on the morning of 15 October, Polly had been found inside the front of their home with partial burns. Her clothes had apparently caught light from the flame of a candle in the early hours of the morning and she had been partly consumed by flames in the front room as the family slept in the rooms above. No one had smelt or heard a thing. Foul play was immediately suspected because her mother's account of the event – and her spotless front room – didn't make sense.

Martha was called as one of the witnesses at Mary Ann's inquest, along with the Favell family, but their accounts were deemed unreliable or forced, and after many days of statements, murder charges were brought upon Polly's mother Jane. Jane was first tried at the Winter Assizes, but the case was thrown out because the evidence against her was poor. But the police were determined to prosecute and offered £100 for new information, which led to her appearing at the Midsummer Assizes in Bedford in 1877. A new witness, Ann Chandler, claimed Jane had admitted to killing Mary Ann after the Winter Assizes and to being haunted by her 'daughter's vision'.[63] Jane claimed she had 'dragged her daughter into the barn and struck her with a stick'. She then dragged her back into the house before she 'poured some oil upon her, and went and sat on a doorstep'. Both doctor witnesses had agreed that the body had been too burnt to have been caused by a candle alone, and another witness stated she had bought 'half a pint of benzoline' (a highly combustible liquid used in lamps) only a week before. This time the jury doubted the evidence and found her not guilty.[64]. Martha had worked with the Favells to create an entirely false narrative of the night Polly died to hide the fact that Jane had caused her death, and that the family had then moved her body to cover up the truth. They were a close-knit family, as thick as proverbial thieves.

In the 1881 census Martha was still working as a straw plaiter, despite hints of foreign plaiting machines poised to revolutionise the industry. Her daughter Emma, now 13, was also working as a plaiter, and Martha had taken a lodger, named Frederick Smith, a plumber. They were living together in America Row (see map on page X), written simply as 'America' in the census. Martha's lodger was in fact Martha's long-term partner and his arrival does appear to coincide with her retreat from the courts and newspapers. They were still living together at the time of the 1891 census and were lodging on Plantation Road with her sister Eliza, who was a 'housekeeper' for head of the household James Barker. Eliza was in a relationship with widower James and 'housekeeper' was the term used in the census for women living with a man they weren't married to; she married him on 21 December 1894.[65]

By the 1911 census Eliza and Martha were still living together, but there was not a man to be found. James, who was nearly twenty years older than Eliza, had sadly died before the 1911 census; the cottage straw plait industry had also died by this stage, on account of 'foreign competition'.[66] It is therefore not surprising that both women were reliant on parish 'out payments', and had been since 1902. For the last twenty years of Martha's life she received payments from the Leighton Buzzard Union along with her sisters, until her death in January 1922 at the age of 76.

Martha's life pivoted around the fortunes and freedoms of the straw plait industry. She started plaiting as a little girl and continued to do so until the industry died. She was argumentative, prone to violence and associated with murder, yet she appears to have held a long-term relationship with a plumber which calmed her criminal behaviour, and she successfully raised two girls. She was part of a close community of women that included her sisters and their wider families. The stereotype of girls and young women losing one or both parents and moving to the big city before sliding into prostitution didn't apply to Martha. She had both parents, never appeared to travel further than the local countryside and was able to support herself by plaiting. Her label as a prostitute was due to her behaviour and to having children out of wedlock – an example of the Victorian double-standard that she appeared to approach head on and stick two fingers up at!

Chapter 6

Very Properly Punished:
Crime and Legislation

I t wasn't a crime to be a prostitute during the Victorian period, but prostitutes were regular visitors to police stations and courts.[1] Their presence in society was feared, but their presence in the legal system was applauded, particularly when high-profile prostitutes received lengthy gaol terms to keep them off the streets. They faced the same legal system as everyone else in the country, but their label as prostitutes set them apart from 'decent society'. It also meant they were subject to additional legislation (for example, for soliciting in the street) and often received harsher punishments for their crimes. These punishments were seen as an important way to curb the growing tide of immoral behaviour, but as the next two chapters will show, punishing prostitutes was not the best way to deal with the issue of immorality.

Apt Punishment

The laws of the nineteenth century were enacted by the police, magistrates and judges as they saw fit, meaning that the punishments received by prostitutes for their crimes could vary considerably across the country – from a 1s fine to transportation. Transportation wasn't just used as an apt punishment for an horrific crime, but as a form of banishment for the most undesirable and corrupting in society. The ultimate punishment was the death penalty which, as you will have read in the death of Betsy Brown, was still in place for the very worst of crimes, but rarely used for women.

The vast majority of crimes associated with prostitutes were petty crimes such as drunkenness, small thefts and being a nuisance in the streets. Anyone accused of a minor offence was seen quickly by local magistrates known as Justices of the Peace at the Petty Sessions. Those accused of greater offences found themselves in front of the Quarter Sessions, consisting of magistrates and a jury, or for the most serious crimes, the Court of Assizes, which was presided over by legally trained London-based judges. The punishments meted out to prostitutes across the country varied on the decision of juries, the whim of a magistrate or judge, previous convictions, the ability of a prostitute to pay a fine, and the legislation at the time. This meant that the two most common crimes of drunkenness, or behaving in the streets as a common prostitute, could result in a fine between 1s and £1 or a gaol sentence from five days to three months.

This discrepancy in sentencing was nothing new to the Victorian era, and earlier attempts at fair punishments had led to a variety of handbooks or guides, most notably Richard Burn's *Justice of the Peace and Parish Officer*, which was used for over a century. But Justices of the Peace were not compelled to follow any guides and could treat immoral women particularly harshly, as we have seen. Rosy Clarke (see her Life Story) is an example of a woman who found herself in a revolving door to the local gaol because the magistrates followed the prescribed legislation exactly as it was written, stopping occasionally to ask what could be done to help her.

There was a pervasive feeling that prostitutes should be 'properly punished' not just for drunkenness, but for their visibly immoral behaviour on the streets. In Huntingdon, Mrs Colliss and another woman known only as Ablett, were both arrested for being drunk and disorderly. They were 'very properly punished by a fortnight's imprisonment in the county gaol'.[2] Visible immorality required visible punishment and nowhere was that sentiment so obvious as a case in Newcastle-under-Lyme, Staffordshire, in 1840. Harriet Higgeson, Sarah Beech and Ann Ashley, 'prostitutes of the lowest grade', were charged with being 'in a disgraceful state of intoxication', as well as behaving indecently and riotously.[3] They were each fined 5s, but Harriet and Sarah 'with a laugh, declared their inability to [pay]'. The magistrate was incensed by their attitude and sent them to the stocks for six hours. They were in high spirits and seemed to be enjoying the punishment, calling out to other people in the marketplace that they were 'The Babes in the Wood'. However, they did start to suffer from their ordeal: 'For three hours neither pain nor shame had taken any effect upon them, but at the end of five hours they loudly petitioned for a change, declaring they would leave the town immediately.' Public shame led to public pain and to public contrition, just as the magistrate had planned.

Indecency

Sitting within the Vagrancy Act (see Chapter 7) was the crime of indecency. If you imagine a Victorian woman, she is almost certainly covered from décolletage to ankle, with a large skirt and probably a bonnet too. Prostitutes working the streets were not afraid to show a little cleavage or raise the hem of their skirts to show an ankle to catch the eye of a passing navvy, and when they had had a few too many mugs of ale in their local beerhouse, they were often guilty of showing more still. Newspaper reports are always vague in their reporting of indecency, but we do get the occasional clue in the records. A few reports help to remind us that prostitutes were not wrapped in layers of petticoats and lengthy modest drawers (closed drawers were thought of as unclean or unhygienic, and it was healthier to be free to the elements until the end of the era), such as the prostitute whose modesty had to be covered by a policeman after passing out on a settle (see page 20).

When Anaïse Marcand, a French prostitute, appeared in front of Mr Pashley QC in Westminster, she was accused of 'walking up and down, holding her petticoats so as to expose above her knee, to attract the attention of gentlemen passing by'.[4] She tried to convince Mr Pashley that she had been wearing drawers at the time, but he could not rule out the possibility that the ones she was wearing in court had been taken from another prostitute with whom she had shared a cell overnight. However, he gave her the benefit of the doubt and Anaïse did not go to gaol for exposing her thighs in the streets.

Indecency covered a much larger range of crimes than exposing intimate flesh including 'urinating in the street and bathing naked in the river to public displays of affection, inappropriate sexual congress and rape'.[5] A prostitute being caught in flagrante with a man in the street could be accused of both indecency and being a prostitute, facing two separate fines for one quick act. This was the case for Catherine Day in 1884 when she was caught having sex on Bridge Street, Birkenhead, and received double the punishment than the man she was with, being found guilty of both prostitution and indecency.[6]

Prostitutes weren't just arrested for exposing themselves on the streets. Annie Grey, 'a showily dressed young woman' was arrested for 'indecently exposing herself upon the Platform' at Southampton train station at one o'clock in the morning.[7] And Mary Evans was caught 'in a very indecent position' in a barn in Congleton, Cheshire, with a man in 1843. Complaints had been made that the barn was being commonly used by trespassers, and Superintendent Hope caught more than he'd expected when he searched there. Mary had already been in front of the bench, so she received three months in gaol for showing a little more than just her thighs.

Transportation: Banishment for the Immoral

Appearing in front of a jury at the Quarter Sessions was a worse affair than appearing at the Petty Sessions because the potential sentences were far greater and the chairmen were not compelled to have any legal training. Transportation was one of the possible outcomes to a trial, with women being sent to Australia for at least seven years, or for the worst cases a life sentence.

The journey to Australia was long and arduous and not everyone made the journey alive. Mary Baker was accused of stealing 'three half crowns' from Edward Crisp when he visited her in a brothel in Norfolk.[8] She was found guilty and sentenced to seven years transportation. She left England on 6 May 1839 on the *Hindustan* and arrived at Van Diemen's Land (now Tasmania) on 12 September the same year. However, Mary's journey had been particularly arduous and she was 'sick the whole voyage'.[9] She was transferred to HM Colonial Hospital in Hobart on her arrival, but never recovered and died on 9 December 1839, aged 23; her seven-year sentence had become a death sentence.

Mary Ann Brett was a prostitute in Burslem, Staffordshire in the 1840s. She was regularly in front of the judges for being a disorderly prostitute and had been guilty of stealing many times. On this particular occasion, in October 1846, Mary Ann was found guilty of stealing 8s 10d by pickpocketing James Brookes in the street and running into Blake's

Spirit Vaults.[10] The moment she stepped out of the building he grabbed her arm and called for the police, but he was then set on by five or six men from the vaults. Amazingly, he was still holding her arm when the police arrived, and in the confusion they were both taken to the station to find out what had caused the affray. The amount Mary Ann stole was not great, but the magistrates were tired of her behaviour and the people she consorted with; this was the final straw. She was sentenced to ten years transportation for a crime that, for others, would have resulted in a small amount of gaol time.

Earlier in the week, at the same sessions, Maria Baker of Bilston had been accused of stealing six sovereigns from John Corser in a 'nest of infamy'.[11] She was acquitted by the jury, but the chairman warned her that if she had been found guilty, he would 'most certainly have sent her out of thē country for at least ten years' for her 'reckless depravity'.

Reverend J. Clare appeared to be particularly harsh when sentencing prostitutes. In 1838 he sentenced three prostitutes at the Staffordshire Summer Quarter Sessions. His dislike of troublesome prostitutes was very clear, describing them as 'a large and dangerous class of females'.[12] He also had no sympathy for the men who 'got drunk and went to places where they could expect nothing else than to get robbed and yet called upon the county to protect them in their folly'. The first prostitute, Ann Brookes, was found guilty of stealing 18s and a tobacco box from the elderly miner who ended up in her bed in the early hours of the morning. Ann was sentenced to twelve months in gaol.

Ann Dunn, of Wolverhampton, was found guilty of stealing a total of three half crowns from Thomas Ward. She had sat with him for a drink and picked his pocket. The amount of money was relatively small, and the theft all the more remarkable for her being in poor health and having 'lost the use of her right hand'. But Reverend Clare had a list of her previous convictions in front of him and described her as 'an old and hopeless offender'. The jury found her guilty and Reverend Clare claimed it would be 'trifling with justice to allow such a person to remain any longer in this country'. She was transported for seven years.

The third prostitute was Jane Platt. She was found guilty of stealing two half crowns and 4s – another relatively small sum – and did so again from a pub. In summing up Reverend Clare stated that:

[prostitutes] went into public-houses under the pretence of selling nuts and other articles and when there singled out their prey, whom they never left until they had robbed them. If they succeeded in obtaining their booty without violence they did so, but if resistance was offered they generally had persons within call to render assistance.

Jane was also sentenced to seven years transportation. Mary Ann Brett, Ann Brookes, Ann Dunn and Jane Platt were being punished for the crimes of their subclass, a class that had been invented to shame the women. None of the women were accused of violence on those occasions, yet their punishments were banishment from the country based on the belief that they would commit further crimes and clog up the judicial system.

The magistrates were fallible, as much as the rest of the population, and their personal lives and beliefs played a part in their sentencing. Reverend Clare was in his seventies at the time of these cases and had recently suffered the loss of his son, who had been horrifically murdered after he had been shipwrecked.[13] Clare was severely depressed and showing signs of dementia too. A year after he sentenced the prostitutes to transportation, he took his own life in the kitchen of the deanery he called home.

Physical Violence

Assaults

The life of a prostitute was often a violent one because women who worked as prostitutes needed to be able to defend themselves from their clients, and potentially fight for any money due to them. They also needed to defend themselves in altercations with other prostitutes and brothel keepers, in fights with their family, and when wrenching themselves from the arms of an arresting police officer.

The majority of the assault cases involved prostitutes as victims, but some were accused of being the aggressor. Assaults covered everything from damaging bonnets (which were an important part of a woman's appearance at the time) to beatings and sexual assaults. Specific prostitute assaults included occasions when they attempted to engage men in sexual activity in an overly aggressive manner as they walked along the street.

Maria Arnold of King Street, Cheltenham, accosted William Jung in the street in 1859, asking him to talk with her. He refused but she continued to harass him. He called for a policeman, who had arrived by the time 'she struck him across the nose with an umbrella'.[14] Maria was given the chance to be bound over to stay away from Mr Jung, but she refused and was initially going to be sent to gaol for six months. However, her defence claimed that she 'was not so right in her mind as she might be.' This hinted at what we might consider a mental health issue today, or what might have been termed madness back then. Her father, they hoped, would give his recognizance for the matter and keep her on the straight and narrow.

Elizabeth Phethean of Back King Street, Bolton, was charged with stabbing her 'companion' William Sharples in 1849. He had been to his father's funeral but didn't want Elizabeth there. When he returned, she started a fight that resulted in him kicking her. In response, Elizabeth stabbed him 'twice in the arm to the depth of about an inch'.[15] She had been accused of stabbing before and therefore found herself gaoled for three months.

Prostitute arguments with other women were plentiful and varied in style. In Cheltenham in 1857 Mary Ann Webb hit fellow prostitute Ann Barnes with a poker in the early hours of the morning. They had been drinking together in the Bath Hotel, but on their way home an argument tipped over into violence when Mary Ann 'inflicted a severe blow' on Ann's head with a poker that she had fetched from her house.[16] They settled the matter between themselves.

Eliza Richardson was well known to Gravesend Police before her attack on another prostitute in the street in 1859. Eliza was said to 'go suddenly behind the other girl and seizing her with both hands, threw her down on the stones and fell on her'.[17] She was very drunk and refused to let go of the other woman until forced to. She received a month in gaol.

In Chesterfield in 1861, Ellen Norton attacked Elizabeth Barber with a 'pint mug of ale' that was broken.[18] They had previously argued, but this time Ellen, fresh from gaol, used the weapon she had at hand. After first throwing the ale over Elizabeth, she then hit her on the temple and cut her face so 'that the cheekbone was exposed'.[19] She was fined £1 and 8s costs, or one month in default.

These women used their physical strength to assault other women, but they also used weapons to escalate an ongoing conflict. The differences in height, weight and strength between women were likely to be negligible, making the fights evenly matched, but weapons allowed them to exert a physical advantage when arguing against men. The weapons could also be used to help defend themselves too, or even to kill.

Murder and Manslaughter

Sarah Swift was only 19 when she killed Elizabeth McGill in 1845.[20] They were both prostitutes in Wapping, a street by the docks in Liverpool. There had been a quarrel earlier in the evening, but the women parted without too much of an issue. However, when they came across each other later in the evening, Sarah wanted to settle her argument with Elizabeth. Elizabeth and her friends noticed Sarah standing nearby, so Elizabeth 'took off her bonnet and shawl, apparently with the intention of proceeding to violence'. They started fighting, with Elizabeth making the first strike. The sailors who were with Elizabeth were leading her away from the fight when Sarah 'ran at her with a knife and stabbed her in the neck'. Elizabeth died quickly, the blade having cut through an artery.[21] After initially being released, Sarah was arrested and charged with wilful murder. A jury decided that she was guilty of manslaughter and she was transported for life.[22]

In another case where a prostitute was transported for life, Hannah Hurd was found guilty of manslaughter after hocussing, or drugging, Thomas Robinson in 1842.[23] He had died in Hannah's brothel and was found to have had a lot of laudanum in his system at the time of death. Hannah was put on trial with her husband Benjamin, but the jury decided that she was the person who had laced Thomas' ale with laudanum to make him easy to rob. She was said to have kept a small bottle of laudanum lodged in her bosom and poured a little into Thomas' glass of ale during the evening, but she did it several times and administered a lethal amount. Hannah was quite open in telling others that she was 'locusting' Thomas, and it was clear that she had not intended to kill the old man, but that is what she did. Hannah travelled to Van Diemen's Land on the *Garland Grove* and arrived there on 20 January 1843.

One case of attempted murder by a prostitute caught the attention of the national press, but for good reason. Elizabeth Roberts lived in Boughton, Chester, and was accused of attempting to kill her daughter Sarah Ann. On the morning of 4 March 1883, Elizabeth returned home in a very drunken state to her friend Martha Antrobus and daughter Sarah Ann, the *Birmingham Mail* suggesting she had been at a 'drunken orgie [*sic*]' all night.[24] Sarah Ann, 14 months old, was sat on a stool by a fire and the moment she saw her mum return, asked for the breast.[25] But Elizabeth was in a foul temper and picked up Sarah Ann by her ankles saying 'You little ----, I'll murder you. I'll burn you to-day', before throwing her onto the fire.[26] Martha (who was hissed at when she first went to court as a witness for the prosecution) had just placed coals on the fire so the flames were low and she pulled the girl off without too much injury.[27] But Elizabeth pulled the child from her arms and returned her to the fire. Again, Martha removed her, but Elizabeth flung her back on a third time. As Sarah Ann was removed, by now suffering some burns to her arm, Elizabeth picked up the kettle and poured boiling water over Martha's arms and Sarah Ann's back. A neighbour, named Brayford, who had also been in the house, took Sarah off the fire, threatening to call the police. Elizabeth responded by threatening to stab her with a knife.

The police came. As Elizabeth was being arrested her words were recorded:

They said I tried to strangle the girl a fortnight ago, but it is a lie. What could I do? I had to keep it myself. Nobody gives me anything to keep it with. I have got to work hard to keep it and it is no joke either. It would be a good job if it did die and I got the rope around my neck for it. Just let me get out of this mess and I am out of Chester, quick.[28]

The jury decided that she was not guilty of attempted murder, but of the far lesser charge of common assault; she was sentenced to a year in gaol.

In Elizabeth's statement she claimed no one gave her anything to 'keep it', meaning she received no assistance from the father or her parish. The father was in prison; he'd been caught poaching and had been sent to gaol for nine months.[29] The newspapers suggested that Elizabeth was originally from Wales and had run away aged 16, so she had no family around her for support; the only support she had had was in Knutsford Gaol. Living in a community of prostitutes was possibly the only reason that she and Sarah were still alive at that point because the community provided childcare, shelter and support. As hated as the haunts or nests of prostitutes were in the press, they were a vital lifeline for women who fell on hard times.

Prostitutes were regularly in court and received a punishment that the magistrate, judge, or jury, thought was most apt. Although it was not illegal to be a prostitute, it was illegal to behave as one. Immoral crimes such as flashing their knees in public or stealing from a man in a brothel both came with the threat of punishment and the certainty of moral shame. These crimes were largely interpersonal, but it was the interpersonal relationships the women had that saved or protected them too. Bad relationships were at the heart of many of the issues in this chapter, the following chapter looks at how legislation was used to control them.

The Drunkard's Children. A drunken scene in a dancing hall with a sly customer eyeing a girl. Etching by G. Cruikshank, 1848. (*In the public domain but from the Wellcome Collection*)

The Rows: 1895 Great Yarmouth Row, Great Yarmouth, Norfolk, Unknown photographer. (*Public domain, via Wikimedia Commons*)

Great Social Evil: John Leech. (*Public domain, via Wikimedia Commons*) The term gay was used as a synonym for prostitute at the time and brothels were occasionally known as gay houses.

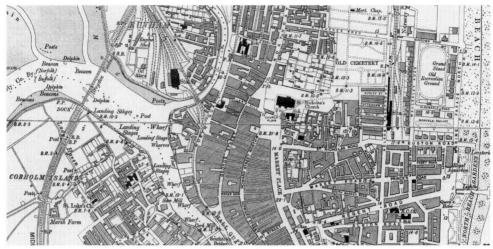

Catherine Thirkettle lived two rows south of The Conge. Her parents originally lived further north on Rampart Row. Both are close to St Nicholas' Church, where Catherine was baptised. Map of Great Yarmouth, 1888-1913. (*Reproduced with the permission of the National Library of Scotland*)

Superintendent Registrar's District *Yarmouth Norfolk*

Registrar's Sub-District *Yarmouth Northern*

1888 . DEATHS in the Sub-District of *Yarmouth Northern* in the County of *Norfolk*

Columns:—	1.	2.	3.	4.	5.	6.	7.	8.	9.
No.	When and Where Died.	Name and Surname.	Sex.	Age	Rank or Profession.	Cause of Death.	Signature, Description, and Residence of Informant.	When Registered.	Signature of Registrar.
8	Twenty seventh January 1888 Workhouse W.S.D.	Catherine Hanson	Female	28 years	Wife of Charles Hanson a Fisherman of Gorleston	Phthisis Certified by J. C. Smith M.R.C.S.	E. Scott present at death Workhouse Yarmouth	Thirtieth January 1888	W.H Perceir Registrar

Catherine Hanson (née Thirkettle) Death Certificate. (*Contains public sector information licensed under the Open Government Licence v3.0*)

Superintendent Registrar's District *Cambridge*

Registrar's District *Saint Mary the Great*

1840. DEATHS in the District of *St Mary the Great* in the Count town of *Cambridge*

No.	When Died.	Name and Surname.	Sex.	Age	Rank or Profession.	Cause of Death.	Signature, Description, and Residence of Informant.	When Registered.	Signature of Registrar.
377	Twenty-fourth of June 1840 at Addenbrooks Hospital	Jane Mackay	female	27	Singlewoman	Burnt to death Accidentally	C.H. Cooper Coroner	Twenty-fourth of June 1840	Peter Bays Registrar

Death Certificate of Jane Mackay. (*Contains public sector information licensed under the Open Government Licence v3.0*)

Examples of flounced skirts. Godey's Ladies: Rijksmuseum. (*CC0, via Wikimedia Commons*)

Elizabeth Ashworth. (*Reproduced by kind permission of Peterborough Archives Service*)

CAMBRIDGE.

(*From a Correspondent.*)

A great proportion of the unfortunate female inhabitants of Barnwell consists of servant girls who have been seduced while in service at Cambridge. These girls, who generally come from the adjoining villages, in the first instance, procure situations in the houses of the tradesmen at extremely low wages. A Cambridge shopkeeper is by no means so extravagant in his own expenditure as the university striplings whom he encourages; and economy, disregarded or detested by him in others, is most dearly prized in himself. He consequently hires a servant girl at the very lowest possible rate of wages, and for his paltry allowance exacts the greatest possible quantity of work in return. The poor devil of a girl is half-starved, knocked about by her vulgar mistress half the day, and bullied on all sides. But these are by no means the worst of her trials. Most of the tradesmen (unless they happen to get discommoned, like "Iniquity" Smith) are in the habit of letting lodgings to the university youths who may not be able to find rooms within their own colleges. These interesting hobbledehoys, of course, make a dead set at the servant girls who attend upon them, and thus Don Juans in ragged gowns carry on their delightful intrigues in comfort under their own roofs.

Under these circumstances the chances are about fifty thousand to one against the girl's virtue (if she has any) coming unscathed from this ordeal. Obliged to wait upon the stripling at all hours, compelled, under pain of losing her situation, to hear every bold and licentious speech it may please the *manly* academician to address to her, allured by the offer of fine clothes, and money—she to whom money is unknown, and whose finery is (like the Misses French) limited to a common cotton gown not over clean, how can we be surprised that she should yield? Again, if the lodger is a "gay" man, Mary, Dolly, or whatever may be her name, is forced to wait at his supper parties, and to hear the language which usually accompanies these entertainments, language to which the utmost obscenity of a brothel, and the strongest rhetorical images of a costermonger, are us snow and purity! The

Satire at the time of Jane Mackay's death explaining how girls became prostitutes. *Satirist; or, the Censor of the Times*, 17 May 1840, p.7. (*In the public domain from www.britishnewspaperarchive.co.uk*)

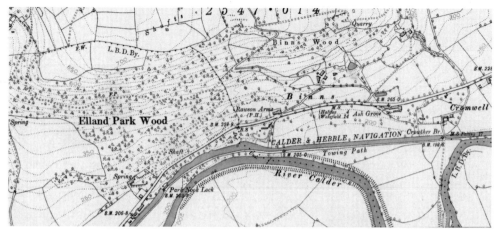

Map of Elland Park Wood showing the isolation of the Rawson's Arms where Hannah/Martha Bentley died, 1894. (*Reproduced with the permission of the National Library of Scotland*)

No.	When Died.	Name and Surname.	Sex.	Age.	Rank or Profession.	Cause of Death.	Signature, Description, and Residence of Informant.	When Registered.	Signature of Registrar.
433	Ninth of January 1844 At Binns Bottom Southowram	Martha Bentley	Female	33 Years	Wife of James Bentley Weaver	Accidental Burning 10 Hours	G. Dyson Coroner Halifax	Eleventh of January 1844	Thomas Mann Registrar

Superintendent Registrar's District _Halifax_

Registrar's District _Southowram_

18**44**. DEATHS in the District of _Southowram_ in the County of _York_

Death Certificate of Martha Bentley showing she died after 'Accidental burning' and lingered for '10 hours'. (*Contains public sector information licensed under the Open Government Licence v3.0*)

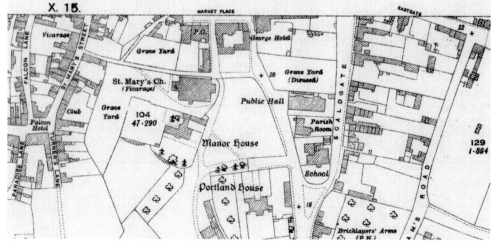

Betsey Brown died in the malting attached to the George Hotel. The George Hotel fronted onto the Market Place to the north and the malting was sited to the south. Map of Whittlesey 1926. (*Reproduced with the permission of the National Library of Scotland*)

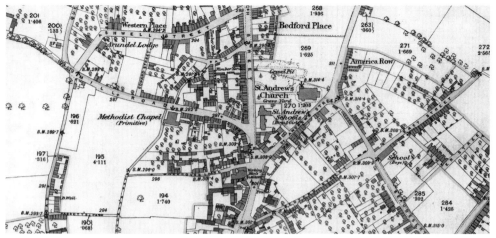

Map of Leighton Buzzard 1892. (*Reproduced with the permission of the National Library of Scotland*)

Map of Whitehaven 1866 showing Peter's Court squeezed in behind houses on Peter Street and the nearby tannery. (*Reproduced with the permission of the National Library of Scotland*)

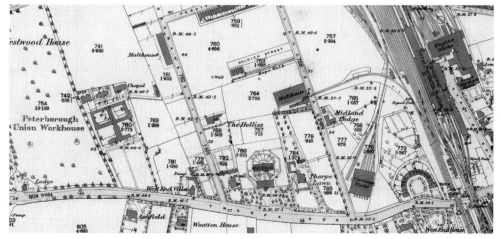

Map of Peterborough showing the workhouse that Susan and Mary Ann Tingey grew up in, the gaol that Susan was sent to and Peterborough North, which they very likely used to leave the city, 1888. (*Reproduced with the permission of the National Library of Scotland*)

Overcrowding and poor living conditions in London 1862; eleven scenes. Wood engraving, 1862. (*In the public domain but from the Wellcome Collection*)

A nobleman and his friends drink with prostitutes in a brothel. Aquatint after H. Dawe, 184-. (*In the public domain but from the Wellcome Collection*)

Susan Tingey's husband: The Great Vance 'a la Française'. (*British Museum, (in the Public domain, via Wikimedia Commons*))

A Harlot's Progress: Plate 5, by William Hogarth. (*CC0, via Wikimedia Commons*)

A SUPPOSED MURDER IN LIVERPOOL.—Yesterday, a woman named Francis Downs, who keeps a brothel in Peter-street, was taken into custody on suspicion of having caused the death of a prostitute, named Martha Surfleet, by striking her with a poker. It appeared that about four o'clock yesterday morning the deceased and prisoner were left sitting on the bed in the room in which they slept; an altercation ensued about some money, and about six o'clock the accused party made an alarm that the deceased was dead, and upon a person, who had previously been in the room, again going in, she found deceased upon the bed, in the same position she had left her, but dead, and a wound appeared above the right eye. The police-officers were called in, and a poker, bearing marks of blood, was found under the bed, with which it is deposed the deceased was struck. On a *post-mortem* examination being made it was found that the deceased, according to one surgeon, had died from congestion of the brain, the result of natural causes; but from the evidence of the other medical gentlemen a doubt existed whether or not death was caused from violence. The Coroner, in order to obtain further evidence, adjourned the case until to-morrow.

INTERESTING GEOLOGICAL DISCOVERY.—The new red sandstone of this district and neighbourhood, has become celebrated in the annals of Geology for the many

The Death of Martha Surfleet, *The Liverpool Standard*, 6 April 1847, p.6. (*In the public domain via www.britishnewspaperarchive.co.uk*)

WEDNESDAY.—(Before Mr. C. Nielsen, mayor.)

THE EXTRAORDINARY DEATH OF A PROSTITUTE ON THE FISH SANDS. —James Gallagher was brought up on remand charged with causing the death of a prostitute named Mary Ann Thornton, on the Fish Sands.—Mr. Supt. Shiels said an inquest had been held on the body of deceased, and a verdict returned to the effect that her death had arisen from natural causes, accelerated by drink. No blame was attached to prisoner, and he (Mr. Shiels) should therefore ask for his discharge.—His Worship (to the prisoner) : You are, then, discharged.—Prisoner : Thank you, sir.—The prisoner then left the court.

FRIDAY.—(Before J. White and Mr. W. Lisle.)

Death of Mary Ann Thornton at Fish Sands, *Darlington and Stockton Telegraph*, 15 July 1871, p.3. (*In the public domain via www. britishnewspaperarchive.co.uk*)

A young distressed woman is standing on the pier of a bridge on the River Thames contemplating suicide. Engraving by T. Godfrey after G. Doré. (*In the public domain but from the Wellcome Collection*)

Chapter 7

Offences Against the Person: Crime and Legislation

W hat shaped the evolving perception of the Victorian prostitute were the many voices calling for their control or protection through books, letter-writing campaigns, public talks and exposés in printed form. Newspapers were crucial in both delivering these views and in providing evidence of the worst prostitute behaviour. The vast majority of these voices belonged to men, but the era also saw the rise of middle-class women who wanted to support and protect prostitutes. Their work in organisations such as the Ladies' National Association promoted the feminist cause and helped to stop the 'prevailing social view of prostitutes as pollutants of men.'[1] As the legislation changed, the lives of prostitutes changed too.

The Vagrancy Act

A large proportion of criminal prostitutes were charged under the Vagrancy Act, and it was this act that named the 'common prostitute'. The Vagrancy Act was created in 1824 with the intention that it would keep the poor in their own parishes and dissuade them from travelling about. The Act punished public immorality, public poverty and public violence of both men and women, but here we will focus on prostitutes alone. The Act aimed to punish prostitutes, 'gypsies' and clairvoyants, people who had no means to support themselves, people sleeping outside, people who looked like they were up to no good outside, people carrying weapons, people exposing themselves, and those who behaved violently when arrested.[2] It stated that for:

> every common prostitute wandering in the public streets or public highways, or in any place of public resort and behaving in a riotous

or indecent manner … it shall be lawful for any justice of the peace to commit such offender … for any time not exceeding one calendar month.

This is the very wording that meant the likes of Rosy Clarke (see her Life Story) and Elizabeth Ann Tremberth yoyoed in and out of their local gaol.

A prostitute would be labelled with a specific term if she was found guilty of a particular offence: common prostitutes found wondering the streets would be termed an 'idle and disorderly person'; if she resisted arrest she would be termed a 'rogue and vagabond' (and subject to three months in gaol); if she'd already been termed a rogue and vagabond and resisted arrest again, then she would be termed an 'incorrigible rogue', which would see her move from a conversation at the Petty Sessions to one at the Quarter Sessions where she could face up to one year in gaol.[3]

If a prostitute was found wandering the streets in a state of intoxication she would most likely be accused of being drunk and disorderly. However, there were many terms that could be used depending on her behaviour which included being drunk and riotous, riotous and wandering, riotous and disorderly, drunk and behaving indecently, drunk and making a disturbance, drunk and soliciting, and many more. The issue was that the women were disturbing others in the street and doing so while drunk.

A specific prostitute crime was wandering the streets for prostitution, often referred to as loitering or importuning, street walking or night walking. Prostitutes walked the busiest streets where they were likely to find the most men, which were often the main thoroughfares, or the streets linking together busy locations such as a market and a dock. The streets crammed with beerhouses and pubs were also very popular with prostitutes, but they were usually arrested there for drunkenness, not importuning passengers for prostitution, because they could do that in the pubs.

There is a difference between urban and rural prostitutes when it comes to drunken arrests, for villages and small towns often only had one main street and at best a handful of pubs. The arrest of drunken prostitutes on streets outside of urban areas was unusual due to the sparsity of the population and police, however prostitutes were arrested in and near pubs for drunkenness, and in barns, privies, outbuildings and fields for all manner of indecent behaviours.

The Larceny Act: Intimate Theft

The Vagrancy Act was not the only legislation that prostitutes fell foul of. Stealing from the person was a crime detailed in the Larceny Act and was most widely associated with pickpockets, often children, reaching into or cutting open pockets in crowded streets. Prostitutes had an unrivalled level of proximity to their clients and were able to steal more valuable items that pickpockets could only dream of. The vast majority of intimate thefts by prostitutes were for money, rings and watches, with the value of the items ranging from a couple of shillings to hundreds of pounds in value. Theft from a man they had been intimate with was a clever crime because many men would not go to the police for fear of damaging their reputation. An Exeter Recorder described these intimate thefts as 'plundering men while in the indulgence of their evil propensities', revealing he had little sympathy for men in these situation.[4]

Some of the thefts from men were very discreet, with the victim not realising he had been robbed until he had left the woman's company, but some prostitutes were too brazen for their own good. Sarah Todd, alias Wilson, was found guilty of 'stealing from the person of Joseph Barton', in Lancaster in 1852.[5] She was said to have accosted Joseph in a narrow alley in the middle of the afternoon where she 'laid hold of him and told him she wanted to speak love to him'.[6] He claimed that he tried to escape from her but 'she thrust her hand into his breeches and pulled down all the buttons'.[7] She fled while he was buttoning himself up, which was when he noticed his purse was missing. He called for the police and Sarah was arrested. In the court case it was revealed that Sarah had only recently arrived in Lancaster from Kendal and was a common prostitute. Unfortunately for her, she had come up against Baron Alderson, a man not known for his tolerance of the lower classes, and prostitutes in particular. On summing up, he 'spoke in terms of such solemnity of the wickedness and demoralisation of prostitution and said that severity was often the greatest leniency'. Sarah was transported for seven years for stealing a purse containing a crown and nine half-crowns (a crown was worth five shillings, so the total value was less than a pound).

Margaret Coates of Carlisle was accused of stealing £1 5s from Peter Wilson after he 'went with her into the Three Crowns Lane' off English Street, on a cold winter's night in 1871.[8] Peter discovered his purse was missing after his encounter and accused Margaret of stealing it. The police searched the lane and discovered it had been hidden there (a common tactic to ensure the offending item is not found on the prostitute if the man immediately discovers his money missing) so she was still charged with the theft. What's amusing about this case is that Margaret tried to bribe the policeman 'with a gold watch if he would "square" the matter'. Amazingly, the judge decided that the purse might have fallen out of Peter's pocket while he was unaware and Margaret was acquitted. Perhaps he had some sympathy for the woman turning tricks in the cold streets of Carlisle in the middle of winter.

Sarah Ann Tilson was accused of stealing the silver watch and guard of William Byfield, a sailor at Terrington near Wisbech in 1855.[9] He'd been to her house for half an hour of fun around midnight and went home to bed. It wasn't until the next morning that he realised his watch was missing and turned up at Sarah's door with a policeman. Sarah followed the same plan as Margaret Coates and hid the watch, but the policeman found it 'in the soil of the privy adjoining the prisoner's house and the guard in the soft water cistern'. She'd thrown it into human waste in her toilet! Sarah was acquitted, almost certainly because William had his excrement-covered watch returned.

Contagious Diseases Acts

If there's one piece of legislation that is associated most with Victorian prostitutes it is the Contagious Diseases Acts (CD Acts) that were first introduced in 1864, extended in 1866 and 1869, and eventually repealed in 1886.[10] The CD Acts were an attempt to reduce the number of soldiers and sailors infected with sexually transmitted diseases by the 'sanitary supervision of fallen women'.[11] These diseases were problematic for the army and navy due to the number of man hours lost to recuperating men, but rather than put the blame on the men and police them, the blame was placed on prostitutes for spreading diseases.[12]

What should be emphasised is that the Act targeted a small number of port and garrison towns, i.e., those with a large population of sailors and soldiers, and was not implemented countrywide. The majority of the towns named in the original CD Act and extensions were in a small pocket of the southeast within easy reach of London, and the others were on the south coast of England and in Ireland. This means that the overwhelming majority of the country was not covered by the Act – or even situated nearby. Prostitutes living elsewhere in the country should have been able to carry on their lives unaffected by the Act, but the legislation was a call to arms for moral reformers across the country who 'claimed success in suppressing street soliciting and brothels throughout Britain in areas where the Acts were not enforced'.[13] The outcry against these immoral women resulted in them being identified and punished for their dissolute behaviour across the country in a way they hadn't before. This was a contagious hysteria over the perceived threat of prostitution and the police's efforts to punish it.

In the locations that fell under the CD Acts the police were required to arrest potentially diseased prostitutes and send them for examination. Women who showed signs of venereal disease were placed in Lock Hospitals until they were 'cured' or no longer showed any signs. If they continued to show signs of disease then they could remain 'for a period not to exceed nine months'.[14] There was no requirement in the rest of the country to have Lock Hospitals, or to put their prostitutes through what was described as 'instrumental rape', but other cities and authorities wanted to appear tough on prostitutes, so a large number of areas had lock wards in hospitals and workhouses.[15]

Some of the lock wards were very short lived, such as the one in Peterborough Infirmary that was first mentioned in 1865.[16] It had been created as a relation of the Peterborough and East Midlands Penitent Females' Home which had opened in 1860. The lock ward was somewhere that women from the refuge could be sent when they needed healthcare, but also a location women could move to from the refuge. However, the aforementioned home only had five inmates, so the need was never very great and it was never referred to beyond the single reference.

The Newcastle Female Penitentiary also had a close relationship with the local infirmary, receiving women from the lock ward to fill their institution.[17] Lock wards were not always popular, nor deemed to be good value for money. At the annual meeting of the Hull Infirmary in 1871 it was suggested that one should be created, but the doctor replied that women with venereal disease who appeared at the door of the infirmary 'were never declined' as they were in other locations.[18] The infirmary board decided to spend their money instead on a 'pathological museum'.

The CD Acts were repealed in 1886 after opposition from influential women like Florence Nightingale, and campaigns from Josephine Butler and Elizabeth Wolstenholme-Elmy, of the Ladies' National Association.[19] This was combined with individual cases of women mistakenly identified as prostitutes and punished (not just in the CD Acts areas); sympathy was growing for women and the disproportionate harshness of regulations around their bodies and lives in general.

The Public Health Act

The Public Health Act of 1875 was broad-sweeping and aimed to improve the quality of water, regulate sewers and drains, improve roads, and regulate lodging houses, slaughterhouses etc.[20] It incorporated the 1847 Towns Police Clauses Act, which covered prostitutes causing an obstruction in the street. The offence had not changed from an earlier 1847 act, per se, but incorporating it into the Public Health Act during the CD Acts era served to elevate the crime and led to undercover policemen attempting to catch women who were soliciting in the streets.

Jane Scrivener found herself in front of the magistrates of the Luton Petty Sessions in February 1876 charged under the new act.[21] She was accused of 'having importuned Superintendent Tydeman for the purpose of prostitution'. Tydeman was working 'in plain clothes' in a sting operation and was approached by Jane who, he claimed, said 'Come and have a walk into some quiet corner: it will be all right: no one will see us: there are no "slops" [police] about now.' The case against Jane was particularly bureaucratic, with Mr Bailey the prosecutor using *Walker's Dictionary* to define what a prostitute was. He stated that 'a prostitute is a hireling, one who is set up for sale, a public strumpet'. The case against Jane was that she had been identified as a common street walker previously, and that general complaints had been made about street walkers in the area. The Chairman wished to ensure that the prosecution was a correct one and pressed to know who made the complaints, but the police refused to divulge the information. Jane's defence, Mr Shepherd, was equally as forceful in questioning witnesses and asking why, if prostitution has taken place 'for a period of some four or five and twenty years', that nothing had been done until then? He claimed that Jane's accusation for prostitution was 'one of the mildest cases that can possibly be', and that she lived with, and worked for, her father. On summing up, the Chairman acknowledged that the Act was only 8 months old and it was possible that women in her situation hadn't yet been informed what the consequences would be if they were caught. She was, therefore, a test case and a warning to the other prostitutes of Luton. She was fined a nominal 10s which was paid by her father, with the Chairman warning that any future cases would be immediately sent to gaol. He wanted Jane to 'consider the life [she had] been leading and to amend it'. Her father was admonished and told to keep an eye on her.

Maria Howard, aged 30, was charged in an almost identical sting operation in Worcester in 1879.[22] Maria was from Dolday in Worcester, but was accused of importuning men at Lowesmoor Bridge on the opposite side of the town. She accosted a plain-clothed Sergeant Summers after the police had been tipped off by a gentleman who had complained about being importuned by a woman there. Maria claimed she was on her way to the nearby station, but it was revealed that she had six previous convictions and was therefore fined 40s, with a fourteen-day gaol sentence if she could not, or would not, pay.

Later Acts: The Turning Tide

By the 1880s campaigners had finally turned the tide on public feeling towards prostitutes. Regulation started to turn people's focus from the prostitutes to the brothel keepers and procurers. The Criminal Law Amendment Act, specifically the Labouchere Amendment of 1885, reflected the change of view from young prostitutes as sinners, to those being sinned against.[23] It raised the age of consent from 13 to 16, and made it illegal to keep any girl under 16 in a brothel. It also became illegal to keep any girl under 18 against her will or the will of her parents, or a woman over 18 against her will. Brothel keepers could be punished for their crimes with up to two years in gaol. The Act also provided the grounds to suppress brothels, with the threat of significant fines (£20 and £40) or gaol time. The Act had been created after the frenzy of the White Slavery scandal in which young girls were taken without consent to brothels both within and outside of England.

Among the evolving national legislation were small local changes in attitude and behaviour. In 1895 Redruth Police placed 'A Warning to Young Men' in the *Cornubian and Redruth Times*.[24] The warning related to a case involving Elizabeth Hicks of Tolgus and John Gribble of Carharrack, who had been caught behaving indecently at the side of a road. Magistrate Mr Lanyon made an important statement that would have been unthinkable earlier in the era and was repeated in the paper:

It was generally taken for granted [that] when a couple are caught indecently behaving in a public thoroughfare that the woman must be arrested, while the man can quietly go away unnoticed. This view was erroneous and [Mr Lanyon] desired that the fact should be made known through the local press.

Prostitution was still an issue in Redruth and the magistrates were determined to sanction both men and woman caught in the act. Lanyon's very clear warning that the rule 'would be stringently obeyed, without regard to the station of the offenders', warned those who might once have been able to erase their name from a situation due to their status would no longer hold that privilege. Lanyon was making the statement public to avoid the potential disgrace of any local gentry and nobility. To the unaware, that would appear to be a magnanimous thing to do; to the wise, it tells us that the young Cornish gentlemen of good breeding were frequently caught with their trousers down and the age of hushed-up public promiscuousness was over.

In 1898 the Vagrancy Act was altered to make it illegal for men to live off the proceeds of prostitution. This meant that husbands could not live off the proceeds of his wife's prostitution (or marry her to do so), and this also applied to bullies, brothel keepers and cohabiting couples. The Borough Police in Leicester came down very hard on 'Six Abominable Scoundrels' who they accused of living off the proceeds of prostitution in the November of 1898.[25] First, Edward Coles was accused of living off the earnings of Cissy Gunby, who was regularly seen working the streets in Leicester. He was followed by Joseph Stodd, who had admitted at the previous Quarter Sessions that he lived off prostitution. He had been living off the earnings of Mary Newberry, who attempted to defend him, but to no avail. William Hunt was said to live with prostitute Annie Green. William Maxwell had previously been fined £10 for running a brothel but denied living off the proceeds of women. He was said to live with a Helen Marriott and was usually seen in the vicinity of prostitutes. Samuel Monk was described as a 'pugnacious-looking character', and 'had lived with three different prostitutes', whom he followed about – although the word pimp was not in the newspaper vocabulary, this was clearly pimp behaviour. His defence was that he intended to marry the woman he was living with. Samuel Oliver had been living with Nelly Simpson, the third prostitute he had lived with. He was described as 'one of these disgraceful men'. Every man received three months in prison with hard labour, the maximum sentence.

The language used in this sentencing is refreshing, describing these male offenders with the same terms that had been used for prostitutes for years. After decades of fighting, legislation was changed to acknowledge that men played their own part in facilitating prostitution and trapping women in the trade.

The Victorian era was a rollercoaster of legislation for prostitutes. Viewed as being at the very route of all Victorian evils and an uncontrollable menace, they were fined, gaoled and banished. As the era progressed they were further demonised, a few targeted locations forcing upon women the indignity of examinations and imprisonment for being diseased. But by the end of the century, young women were better protected from sexual harm and abuse than they ever had been and the persecution of Victorian prostitutes was finally on the wane; at last, the people who pulled girls and women into the trade were the ones being properly prosecuted. The tide had turned.

Life Story: Rosy Clarke

Whitehaven is situated on the Cumbrian coast, looking west over the Irish Sea. Its location has made it a great harbour and shipbuilding site, and along with its trade in coal and other goods, it was said to be 'the most important seaport in Cumberland'.[26] Historically, the town was seen as one of hard-working men, industry and progress; not much thought was given to the women who lived there. Rosy Clarke was one of the noisiest and rudest woman who ever lived in Whitehaven and her story is one the town would probably choose to forget. But Rosy's life was, of course, linked to the large numbers of men living in Whitehaven, and if we can find a place to remember the men, we should find a place for the women too.

Rosy was born Rosanna or Rosannah, and was also known as Rose, Rose Anna, and Rose Ann. It is very difficult to tie down her exact birthplace, date, or age due to inconsistent records. The earliest record appears to be the 1841 Whitehaven census, where she was named Rose and was living with her family on Charles Street. It claims she was 2 years old and born in Ireland, making her birthdate 1839. The Clarkes were part of a large community of Irish migrants living in Whitehaven. Figures from the 1851 census calculated there were over 4,000 Irish people living in the town, which was more than Carlisle and Cockermouth combined (around 3,000 together), and potentially more than the rest of the county combined.[27] The Whitehaven population was said to be below 20,000, meaning Irish immigrants made up around 20 per cent of the population of the town.[28]

The family moved to Whitehaven after Rosy was born but before the arrival of her sisters, twins Catherine and Ann, who were 2 months old at the time of the census, and died at the age of 1 and 8 respectively. Sadly, her father James, a labourer, died a few months after Ann in 1849, leaving her mother a widow with five children to raise. She worked as a charwoman along with her lodger Ruth Barnes, and was supported by her eldest son John, labouring like his father had. Rosy would have been roughly 10 when he died, but was still apparently at school in the 1851 census.

Rosy made her first appearance in the *Whitehaven News* in 1859 as Rose Clarke. She was roughly 20 years old and lived with her family in Peter's Court, a collection of slums squeezed between Peter Street, Queen Street and Charles Street, and close to the tannery (see map on page x). The tiny family home which she shared with her mother, her brother James, and lodger James Marsden (very likely her mother's partner) would have felt very small in the dark nights of December, so Rosy had headed out to look for a little comfort. She got drunk and was lured towards Miss Harris' confectionary shop on nearby Queen Street. By this point, Rosy was working as a charwoman with her mother and was very unlikely to have had the money to buy sweet treats. She was also foul-mouthed and not afraid to threaten and intimidate to get what she wanted. The *Whitehaven Post* reported that she had 'broken a glass globe and destroyed a quantity of fancy goods', belonging to Miss Harris.[29] This wasn't an accidental break, this was a deliberate break of the globe.

Rosy didn't hang around and wandered down George Street towards the harbour, ending up on Tangier Street. There she got into an argument with another woman and by the time the police caught up with her she was wrestling the bonnet from the woman's head. She appears to have avoided gaol but was fined 5s for drunkenness and ordered to pay Miss Harris 30s for the damage she caused in her shop.

Seven months later she was back in front of the bench, who demanded she found sureties to keep the peace for three months or she would be sent to gaol for the same time.[30] She was described as a 'notorious character', strongly suggesting she had been far from a model citizen since her drunken escapades in December.

A year later, in 1861, she was in court in a case worthy of the scandal-hungry papers. She had appeared in front of the magistrates before then, but this was the first account that had found its way to the papers. This time, accused of being drunk and disorderly in the streets on a Sunday morning, she took offence at Sergeant Little when he was called to the stand. She called out that he should tell the truth and said, 'it is a sin to let him speak. It is a wonder his "mufstach" does not fall off when he speaks.'[31] To which the room laughed. He claimed he'd told her to go home to which she replied, 'it is an untruth. How durst you stand there you ugly _____?' She continued to argue with his account of the event saying, 'It is a wonder the place does not sink down, there are so many lies told in it.'

Sergeant Little explained to the bench that she had been arrested only a few days before and they were at a loss with what to do with her. When she was in the police cells, he claimed, she 'seize[d] hold of the policemen and pull[ed] them about like a mad person'. This had been her thirteenth call before the bench and it was far from being her last.

Through her continued harassment of the police sergeant, we also learn that she had been working at 'the mills'. At the time there were 'flax and tow spinning mills', but the pay was poor and she was rather lazy according to the sergeant.[32] Rosy did not like the inference and shouted 'oh; you ugly _____. By _____ if I had my will...', before she was silenced by the bench and told she'd be fined 20s or gaoled for three months in Carlisle. 'I can stand that on my head easily,' she said with delight. She then jumped out of the dock and grabbed the policeman's hair as she was being led out.

Charged with drunkenness at the beginning of February 1862, she was sent back to Carlisle Gaol for three months.[33] In August she appeared with her friend Ann Edgar after being drunk on Strand Street, another street running parallel with the harbour and full of pubs and beerhouses. This time she was referred to as 'the eminently notorious Rosy Clarke', and was identified as a prostitute for the first time.[34] She was accused of stealing sixpence and a medal from a man, but he failed to turn up to court – very common with prostitute thefts – and so she was charged only for drunkenness. She can't have been gaoled for long, because by the end of September 1862 she was again called to the bench with Ann Edgar, this time referred to as an 'eminently disorderly prostitute'.[35] She was drunk again and given three months gaol time. On her way out of court she 'utter[ed] filthy language and offer[ed] a privilege to all in the court which it was not likely anybody would avail themselves of'.

By January 1863, only a few days free from gaol, she was in front of the bench again – her sixteenth appearance – for behaving badly on Duke Street.[36] She went straight back in for another three months. She was back in front of the bench in August in tears after being arrested for being drunk at 1 o'clock on a Sunday morning.[37] She was desperate to be forgiven and sobbed until she was released, thankfully for her, without charge. This was her nineteenth call to the bench. She was back a few days later for the same offence and again handed three months in Carlisle Gaol.[38]

Around six months after her release in April 1864 she was back again. This time she was drunk on Strand Street and being threatened with arrest if she didn't go home. Thankfully a man walked off with her and the arrest was averted. Until, that was, they reached the end of the street and she 'knocked the man down' and started an argument.[39] It took three policemen to take her away. At the court it was revealed that she had only been released from gaol that morning and she had now spent twenty-nine months there.

The magistrates spent some time considering what to do with her. It was clear that continually sending her to gaol for three-month stretches had no effect on her behaviour, but their sentences were curtailed by legislation; she was given three months again. However, she added to it by attacking a policeman on her way out of the dock and then offering 'the most filthy and abusive language ever heard in a court of justice'. Two months was added on for the assault.

It was after that visit to the bench that she found her name in the paper yet again, but this time not of her own doing. A gentleman identifying himself as 'One of the Higher Class' wrote a letter to the *Whitehaven News*.[40] In it he made assertions that poor people should remember their places in society and, on the subject of the poor cart drivers being fined by the magistrates, stated: 'They have no business to be poor. If they cannot afford to keep good fat horses they have no right to keep horses at all. As to how they are to live, that's no part of my business or the magistrates either.' He told the magistrates to fine 'the blackguard cart drivers', the 'poachers, salmon priggers [thieves] and Rosy Clarke's [*sic*] and such off-scum of society. They seem to me to be here for no other purpose than fining.' His epistolary rant provides a fascinating window into the views of the upper echelons of society, who believed that those lower in society should do as they were told and accept their lot. He also made Rosy Clarke a synonym for wayward prostitutes, which likely delighted her!

By December of the same year, she was back in front of the magistrates. She was drunk again and, in the cold of a December Saturday night, was 'exposing her person' on the street.[41] She was sentenced to two months of hard labour and the paper claimed it was her twenty-fourth conviction. She was still only 25 years old.

By 1865 Rosy seems to have started playing the system a little more. Rather than travelling back to Whitehaven from Carlisle she remained there to get drunk.[42] She was described as 'an importation from Whitehaven', the headline calling her 'A Regular Gaol Bird'. In court there was a small disagreement as to whether she had been to gaol twenty-four or twenty-seven times. Naturally, the woman who claimed she was two or three years younger than she was (she regularly gave her birth date as 1842), was convinced she had only been to gaol twenty-four times, whereas her official record was twenty-seven. She was allowed time to leave the town rather than go to gaol, but given her record, it's very likely she headed back in. No records have yet been found for her escapades in 1866, but she certainly spent much of her time in gaol.

In April 1867 Rosy was involved in a case of 'Bonneting and Robbing a Man' with her friend Catherine Keswick, another prostitute of equal infamy.[43] The pair came across an old man, John Richardson, in Whitehaven in the middle of the afternoon. They 'shoved his hat over his eyes, knocked him down and took the money from his pocket'. In a rather selfless act Rosy tried to take all of the blame herself, but witnesses saw both women knock him down and rob him and they were both charged.

By November 1867 she had returned to Carlisle and was classed as a nuisance. She was sent to gaol for another month for drunkenness, after previously promising to leave Carlisle.[44] By then she was said to have thirty-three convictions, meaning she had added another nine convictions between 1865 and 1867.

By 1868 her sentences started to increase in length. On 7 April, she was convicted of being an incorrigible rogue and received a year in Carlisle Gaol.[45] Barely two weeks after her release in 1869 she was convicted of being an incorrigible rogue and vagabond – she was, of course, not in Whitehaven and had no home to speak of – and given another year in gaol. The magistrates had found an answer to the question about what should be done with Rosy Clarke, and that was to give her longer sentences in gaol. In the Calendar of Prisoners, it revealed that her first crime was recorded in 1857 (she would have been 18) and she had been 'twenty-nine times committed as a disorderly prostitute'.[46]

It was in 1870 that Rosy received her biggest punishment for her greatest crime, that of grievous bodily harm. She had spent much of her life standing in front of magistrates at Petty Sessions hearings, but this time she was at the Midsummer Quarter Sessions, which comprised of thirty-two magistrates and twenty jury men. On 18 October, six months into her year-long prison stay, she 'had committed an offence against the Gaol Discipline Act', for which her punishment was to be 'placed in a dark cell'.[47] Warder Thomas Wright was tasked with taking her to the cell, but she would not go. We know from previous stories that she often put up a fight when facing punishment and had needed several men to manhandle her to where she was supposed to be. She was incredibly violent and 'when she had reached the bottom of the stairs, seized the warder by the calf of the leg and bit a piece of flesh out of it'. So significant was the bite that Thomas needed treatment for three weeks. With a gaol full of witnesses and thirty-two previous visits to gaol, she had pleaded guilty and was given five years penal servitude. She thanked the court for the sentence, 'but immediately afterwards began struggling with the warders and violently resisted being taken downstairs'. Interestingly, the Calendar of Prisoners recorded the gaoler's name as David Wright and claimed she had been convicted thirty-four times 'as a drunk and disorderly person and twice for felony'. All of her key details have a fluidity of truth to them.

Rosy did not remain in Carlisle Gaol for her punishment, but was moved to Millbank Prison, London, which is where she appeared in the 1871 census. She claimed to be 29 years old, of no profession, and from Whitehaven.

We might have expected Rosy to remain in gaol until 1875, but she was released early on licence and headed north. In February 1874 she travelled to Hebburn, Durham. Her brothers Peter and James were working in the coal mines there and were living together with their mother, Isabella. The family might have wished to leave the shadow of their sister's reputation and start a new life on the other side of the Pennines, but unfortunately for them, Rosy arrived on her release and got drunk and 'very riotous'.[48] She was charged on 13 February but absconded, returning at the end of April to face her fine of two shillings and sixpence.

The reason she had fled and returned was revealed in the Whitehaven press. The Gaol Committee had been alerted that Rosy was released on licence after only three years and five months and wanted answers. Because she had been released on licence, her arrest in Jarrow could – or should – have meant a return to prison, hence her fleeing, but her return to Whitehaven caused local bureaucrats to ask why she was free.

Rosy married at the end of 1874 to miner Edward Nicholson in Sunderland, but this was no fairy-tale ending to her life of drunken arguments. She was charged at Jarrow Petty Sessions with being drunk on 8 December, and said she'd only been married a few weeks. Her sister (probably sister-in-law) pleaded for her to be allowed home because she relied on her help and explained that Rosy's husband 'was not the best'.[49] But she had already skipped bail and been charged a few times that year with drunkenness. Her sister offered to pay her 10s fine, but she chose to go to gaol instead. On 10 February 1875 she was sent to gaol for a month for being drunk and disorderly and was referred to as 'Rosanna Nicholson alias Clark' [sic].[50] She was described as 'a returned convict and has often been in the lock-up on this charge'. She had to be taken to the police station in a barrow.

She appeared in front of the Hebburn Police Court in October 1880, receiving fourteen days of hard labour for drunkenness.[51] By the 1881 census she was in gaol in Durham again. She gave her name as Rose Ann Nicholson, aged 36 (it was more like 42), and she claimed she was from Whitehaven. Rose Ann appeared to be her preferred nomenclature in Hebburn and she appeared many times under the name. Her census incarceration was not a long one and she was back in the streets drinking by 25 June. But Rose was showing more signs of distress than her drinking and also attempted to end her life. She was not charged for the attempt, but she did receive another two weeks for drunkenness.[52] In June 1882 she received yet another week for drunkenness.[53] In July she popped over the River Tyne to Tynemouth, perhaps enjoying a little trip to the beach, but she received another three days for drunkenness.[54]

On 1 December 1884, Rosy or Rose Ann made her thirty-sixth appearance at the Hebburn Police Court.[55] She was, of course, drunk and disorderly, and was given two weeks of gaol time. The chairman's comments stand out as he said, 'it is shocking to see so much drunkenness in the midst of such distress.' He also said she 'was well known in Jarrow, Wallsend, Willington Quay and other places on Tyneside and her convictions number about 100'. It is awful to look back with modern eyes and know that there are many treatments and much support available now that could have helped Rosy, but it is at least a little reassuring that the magistrates recognised that she was in distress and not just a nuisance.

She continued to appear before the magistrates through the 1880s and into the 1890s, and in the 1891 census with Edward in Hebburn, but she is difficult to trace after 1894. Due to her many names and varying birth date and location, it is difficult to find a death record for her, but the search will continue.

Rosy's life highlights the difficulties in trying to locate and age prostitutes in official documents. It also underlines the failures of the legal system as she found herself in a continual cycle of arrest, gaol and release. The only part of the system that acted as a deterrent was the dark cell, the thought of which caused her anger to bubble up and result in an assault on a warder, but gaol itself was little threat to her and any promises to change her behaviour were never actioned. She drank heavily, she swore, she threatened, she attacked and at times rampaged through her life. We know she married, but her husband was not a nice man. How her final days played out is yet unknown, but with a seam of violence and drinking throughout her life, it was probably not pleasant.

Chapter 8

Anchorless: Travel and Transiency

You might easily be forgiven for thinking that Victorian prostitutes lived their whole lives in a very small area, and for many, such as Martha Baines, that was entirely true. But the expansion of the railways and the improvement of roads allowed people to travel long distances without spending days or weeks meandering through the countryside. The ability to easily and quickly travel across the country opened up opportunities and experiences that had not been available to people at the beginning of the century and prostitutes made the most of them.

The Victorians' love of documentation also left a legacy that identified where people were. They were identified every ten years in the census and when they entered a workhouse, a prison, a courtroom, got married, had children and more besides. It's therefore possible to identify when and where prostitutes lived, worked and moved around. We can identify both micro and macro movements – house to house and across towns, counties, countries etc. – and we can identify journeys for pleasure, for work, by force and for escape.

Transiency

Many prostitutes were born into a world of poverty, some living in streets where all of their neighbours were equally poor and illegal behaviour was a way of life – a way to survive. In Charles Booth's Poverty Maps of London, he colour-coded the streets based on the class of the people who lived there and identified the worst streets with a thick black line denoting the 'Lowest Class. Vicious, semi-criminal.'[1] Every town and city had areas of deprivation and illegal behaviour and many people found themselves trapped in these 'Lowest Class' streets for want of money, employment, or escape. However, the occupants of these streets rarely remained in one place for long, moving on to the next miserable room or bed as need or necessity dictated.

Elizabeth Ashworth, also known as Betsey, spent her childhood in Yaxley, Huntingdonshire, living with her family in a little cottage on the very edge of the village and the edge of the Fens. She married John Ashworth and moved to Peterborough in 1874. Shortly after, she after was convicted of her first crime. This set off a permanent transiency between gaol and insecure accommodation, both with and without her husband. Each census and arrest captured her living in a different location in Peterborough in Boongate, a location synonymous at the time with prostitution and thieves. Analysis of her behaviours shows movement between her family in Yaxley, the police and court buildings in Peterborough, as well as the streets of Boongate. Police records reveal that Betsey was argumentative and violent (she threatened to stab her mother on one visit to her parents), and moved around as a consequences of her actions. She was always recorded with a roof over her head, but the locations were a mixture of gaol cells, slums and lodging house rooms. Betsey bounced from one location to the next, causing chaos wherever she went and never finding a secure home for more than a few years at most due to her constant arguments, violence and frequent returns to gaol.

Betsey's transiency between lodgings and institutions was replicated by prostitutes across the country. Catherine Thirkettle moved around the mitochondrial streets of Great Yarmouth before dying in the workhouse. Rosy Clarke was in and out of prison due to drunken and violent behaviour. She lived most of her life in the streets of Whitehaven, leaving only to escape or to find comfort from her family. Their lives were unstable, their lodgings insecure, yet their lives outside of the legal system were contained within a very small area. They travelled only when forced to.

A study of prostitutes in India stated that a failure of 'family and marital ties' could 'generate a "process of anchorlessness"', which, 'along with the lack of ability to provide for themselves due to poverty and illiteracy', meant the women were forced into prostitution to survive, exactly as the Victorian women were.[2] This anchorlessness was temporary for the vast majority of Victorian prostitutes, but for some, like Betsey, it was a perpetual state. Despite this breakdown in relationships, these anchorless women stayed close to the people who were most important to them, to streets that were familiar and to friends and associates that helped them to survive. The value of a tab at the local pawnbrokers or beer shop should not be underestimated for someone who has very little. The comfort or security of living next door to family, even if they quarrelled, was something that would make a miserable life liveable.

Migration

For many prostitutes their route into prostitution rose entirely out of the hope of a better life. They had left their home and flocked with thousands of others to larger urban centres – something that changed the face of the entire country. As the Industrial Revolution created new jobs in industries in towns and cities, rural economies stuttered and stalled, which led to a vast movement of young workers into urban settings hoping to find work, friends, husbands and wives. However, a large number of women discovered the bitter reality of low paying domestic work and mistreatment, and left their employment, thereby finding themselves 'without house, home, or guide in some busy town, with which [they were] perhaps altogether unacquainted'.[3] With ties to their family severed on account of their newfound independence and their distance from home, they found themselves vulnerable and at the mercy of anyone who could offer them work.

People working to rescue prostitutes identified that a considerable number of the girls they were in contact with had migrated from a rural to urban location, rather than being from the existing urban population, and found themselves quite helpless. A warning letter from Mr Talbot of the National Society for the Protection of Young Girls was published in local newspapers in 1867, in the hope of 'preventing many young and innocent girls from being entrapped into a life of degradation and misery' in London.[4] However, the chance of being duped or abandoned when undertaking rural to urban migration was true in any town or city, and in any part of the country.

In Cornwall, girls left rural mining communities to find work in towns, congregating in large numbers in Redruth. The same was true for young women travelling to Plymouth where it was claimed that they 'were mostly country girls from the mining districts.'[5] There was vocal concern about country girls flooding into towns, which was repeated in the papers for Weymouth, Liverpool, Blackburn, Leeds and Sheffield, but it was a reality for most larger towns and cities.

It should be noted that not all towns were flooded by women from the countryside, nor were there complaints about it. Stamford, for example, was a small town during the nineteenth century. It did not grow as other towns did and was barely touched by the progress of industry. As a pleasure town previously reliant on coaching trade on the Great North Road (now the A1), it suffered greatly when the railways arrived and the mainline bypassed the town. It therefore remained a small town at the centre of an agrarian economy through the Victorian era. Workers moved in and out of the town and countryside as seasonal needs dictated and as they had for centuries. Villagers and rural workers visited the town for markets to sell their animals and goods, and men spent some of that money on drink, a good meal and a night with a prostitute.

In Peterborough, there was an increase in prostitutes in the second half of the era, but again, the numbers were not considerable. This is likely to be because of the enormous influx of men working on the railways and the brickmaking industries. The city's population ballooned, but long rows of neat terraces were erected for the railway workers meaning that there was potentially a man with a new home and a good wage available for any single woman travelling in from the country. Although Peterborough was the poorer of the two neighbouring towns, the wages and homes of the average worker there meant that it was a better choice for a young woman looking for a husband and a settled life.

The situation was very different in Liverpool in the 1880s; so many prostitutes were living there that they were spilling out into neighbouring districts. The Chief Constable of Birkenhead was concerned that prostitutes were ferrying over the Mersey from Liverpool at night and getting drunk and disorderly on his streets, rather than those of Liverpool.[6] Neighbouring New Brighton suffered the same problem, with Liverpool prostitutes being arrested for drunk and disorderly behaviour there on a Sunday evening.[7]

Not only was Liverpool seeing a significant number of migrants following the rural to urban trend, but as a port city Liverpool received a large quantity of immigrants from Ireland, Scotland, Wales, and in smaller numbers from the nearby Isle of Man, according to one very irate correspondent in a local newspaper.[8] They had all arrived in the hope of finding work and benefiting from the many opportunities available in the vastly expanding city, so it is not surprising that the city was full to bursting.

Liverpool wasn't the only location to welcome immigrants; all of the big cities, particularly those with ports, received lots of enthusiastic incomers. However, moving to England from other parts of the British Isles they often found they were unwelcome and subject to racism or micro-aggressions, from name calling to refusing to acknowledge them as locals.

London received the largest number of migrants, seeing its total population swell to 6.5 million people by the end of the era. The pull towards the vast metropolis was the greatest, and in consequence it also appears to have had the largest number of prostitutes, if the frankly ridiculous estimates from contemporary writers were even vaguely close to the truth. However, the pull to London was not absolute and prostitutes also migrated away from the city, either on tramp, or in the hope of better work away from the fetid slums, some ending up in other prostitute strong-holds such as Portsmouth, or in smaller towns and cities such as Worcester and Stamford.

This small-scale migration away from London was replicated in all the major cities as prostitutes constantly looked for a better life. Jane Moorcroft had been working as a prostitute in Manchester in 1866, but had moved to nearby Ashton-under-Lyne where she was identified as living in a brothel.[9] Likewise, Margaret Clark moved from bustling Bradford to quieter Louth in 1846, possibly lured by the entertainments of the fair, where she was gaoled for one month for indecent behaviour.[10]

Travelling for Pleasure

Prostitutes loved a bit of fun, with lots of them appearing in the papers after visiting pleasure fairs, hiring fairs and shows. They went along with thousands of other people, swelling often small communities with hordes of interlopers. Police reports relating to these events across the country frequently emphasised the origin location of the miscreant to disassociate the town with the 'certain class of suspicious looking strangers'.[11] The presence of large numbers of thieves and prostitutes was feared by the organisers and the police, and there was always much celebration when the events took place without too much criminal activity. In Kent in 1860 they had predicted large numbers of prostitutes and pickpockets etc., and drafted in scores of extra police to help manage the unruly crowds, as they did in Louth at their November fair, where they celebrated their 'excellent and well-disciplined police' after a peaceful event.[12]

At a meeting of the Wenlock Farmers' Club in 1861 there was a talk on the evils of hiring fairs.[13] Reverend Edward Jackson claimed that young people could 'date their fall from virtue on Hiring Day'. He claimed: 'when the business of the day [had] drawn to a close the pleasures of the evening commence[d]'. And in an Attenborough-esque description of prostitutes, stated:

> Each female selects her male companion for the evening, whose duty it is to see her to her distant home at the close of the amusements in the darkness of the night … The very devils in hell would delight and be satisfied with the orgies and revel that follow.

This places the behaviour firmly on the 'female', who selected her victim as if she were a spider and he a fly trapped in her web of immorality. Yet there were countless other stories of young women who had gone in search of employment and were assaulted or tempted down a path of immorality at the same events.

Melton Mowbray was the site of an enormous annual hiring or statute fair to which prostitutes flocked in the hope of having a little fun and making some money. The fair featured everything from 'photographers, stall-keepers and general "catch pennies"', to 'a long range rifle gallery', roundabouts, and 'Wombwell's Royal Windsor Castle Menagerie'.[14] Mary Taylor was arrested there in 1868 accused of 'attending Melton Statues for purposes of committing a felony'.[15] She was discharged following her promise to move on – a very common promise for prostitutes far from home.

Melton's central location appears to have been a popular stopping point for travelling prostitutes and the magistrates were keen to identify them as being from elsewhere. Kate Morgan of Coventry and Sarah Whitaker of Godmanchester were both arrested for poor behaviour in Melton in 1875 and Mary Smith from Barnard Castle (150 miles away) was found drunk there the following year. Although Melton is close to the Great North Road, it would have been a sizable diversion for either Sarah or Mary, who might have been travelling along it, however it had a well-connected railway station with lines running north-south and east-west, so it's possible they arrived by rail.

Escape

Some girls and women left their homes to escape their situation and either knowingly, or accidentally, ended up in a brothel. Esther Ross was only 14 when she ran away from home in 1849.[16] She lived in Broughton, Nottinghamshire, and fled to nearby Nottingham. Esther was arrested in August, having been away from her home for a month. She was living at 'a bad house in Wheat Sheaf-yard' with Joseph and Phoebe Gregg who had been in Nottingham for only two weeks. We know, therefore, that Esther hadn't arrived and immediately moved to their brothel, but had moved there after two or three weeks in the city and that prostitution was not her ultimate intention when she fled.

Mary Beddows was 15 when she ran away from home in Wolverhampton. She headed east and ended up in the home of 18-year-old Alice Bamford in Walsall. After living there for a while and losing her virginity to Alice's partner, she learnt the life of a prostitute and moved to Ann Smalley's house. But Mary was 'taken ill [and] had to be removed to the workhouse', where the story came to light.[17] It was 1893, so Alice and Ann were arrested for procuring and harbouring a girl under 16. Neither were found guilty of procuring her because Mary had apparently claimed she was 16, but both were found guilty to harbouring her. Alice received twelve months in gaol and Ann, who was 47 (and described as an old woman!) was given eighteen months.[18]

When Caroline Brown argued with her mother in a Yorkshire village, she ran away north to Stockton where she began 'living by immorality'.[19] She was 'about 18' and accosting men in the street at night. On this occasion the police attempted to contact Caroline's friends so that she could be returned to a respectable life.

Other women were travelling to avoid a terrible trauma and/or an abusive partner or family member. Catherine Morris, also known as 'Welsh Kit', had migrated from Wales to England to find work. She had lived for a while in Wolverhampton which is where she met James Sones. They moved together across the country to live in Ipswich, Suffolk, close to James' family. There they had a young daughter, Eliza, who died in March 1851 after her clothes set alight when she was sitting alone by the fire.

The couple were still living in Ipswich at the time of the census a few weeks after Eliza's death, but Catherine ended their relationship shortly after and moved back to Wolverhampton, with an angry James hot on her heels. James had been accused of assault and theft several times before and later admitted he hadn't coped well with the death of his daughter. He couldn't cope with Catherine leaving him either, so he tracked her down in Wolverhampton. He hung around the pub she was drinking in with the excuse that he wanted her to return some items of his that she had kept. She reluctantly agreed to go with him to her lodgings, but they never made it there. After barely a word spoken to her, he slit Catherine's throat in the yard at the back of the pub, mortally wounding her. She died several days later after providing a written and oral statement that he was her killer. He was found guilty of manslaughter and transported for life.

Some prostitutes lived their lives in a small area, bouncing from unpleasant situation to unpleasant situation. Others were able to travel long distances in the hope of fun, escape, or a new life. These longer journeys gave the women opportunities to earn some money and meet new people, but it occasionally led to their abuse or even their death.

Chapter 9

Like Any Other Commodity: The Traffic of Victorian Girls

T his chapter focuses on the exploited migration of women and girls for prostitution across England and from European countries. In the second half of the nineteenth century a large number of women migrated for employment opportunities across Europe, which included sex work. This movement was known contemporaneously as 'traffic' in the newspapers, a term that applied to all types of migration, not solely to the sex trade.

With such large numbers of people migrating, there were opportunistic individuals ready to exploit or manipulate those with hope at their heels. The terms 'procured' and 'decoyed' were used to describe women and girls being lured into the sex trade unknowingly or unwillingly, but what wasn't used was the word trafficked. Trafficking is a more modern term and can be problematic when discussing historical behaviour. In an article for the *Journal of Women's History*, Julia Laite and Phillipa Hetherington highlighted the 'malleability of the term', and the fact that 'its precise definition and parameters remain blurry and imprecise'.[1] Its use as a legal or political term is open to interpretation and change, and the idea of what it means to be trafficked can vary from one person or organisation to another.

Similarly, some people might consider trafficking of sex workers to only relate to movement between countries or across long distances, and disregard anything within a country or county. However, women could be (and can still be) transported across relatively short distances and come under the definition of traffic, trafficking, or enslavement. The United Nations' current stance on trafficking states: '[e]xploitation can take place in a victim's home country, during migration or in a foreign country'.[2]

There are a number of books that claim that '"traffic in women" has historical precedent in the late nineteenth century', but this disregards a large number of women who were being exploited in the middle of the century.[3] There were plenty of newspaper accounts that identified a trade in young migrant women and voiced their concerns at the exploitation of girls, going both to and from the continent and within the country.

Domestic Traffic

There are clear examples of the traffic in women in the 1840s and 1850s, both on a national and international level. London features heavily in discussions on the exploitation and migration of women for sex, but it's important to view the issue from a country-wide perspective because the issue was not isolated to the main metropolis.

In Worcester in 1858, two nameless girls of around 13 or 14 years of age were found in the company of Mary Ann Griffiths, a prostitute. The girls were originally from Dudley but had met Mrs Griffiths in Birmingham, under 10 miles away, where she had persuaded them to travel to Worcester with her. Mary was visibly drunk and was behaving disorderly in the streets, which caught the attention of PC Berridge. He was immediately suspicious that the two young girls at her side had been procured for prostitution, and when he was questioning them Mary was quite abusive, so he locked her up and took the girls to safety. Mary was fined 5s for drunkenness and the girls were 'by the generosity of a gentleman … sent home to their friends'.[4] There is no indication of whether the girls were exploited by Mary, but with her status as a prostitute, the police constable's concern, and the gentleman paying for their return home, we can be certain that she had at the very least intended to exploit the vulnerable girls. The girls didn't travel far – less than 10 miles to Birmingham and around 25 miles to Worcester – but by removing the girls from Birmingham, where their families thought they were, Mary loosened any ties to their home and potential rescue. Although she was taking them from a large urban area to a smaller one, she was taking them to a town they didn't know that was also a prostitute hotspot, and her intention was clear.

In the same year, the authorities in Blackburn were concerned with the amount of prostitution in the town, so they decided to look at the issue in the national context. They knew that big metropolises were 'alive to the evil of having so many "unfortunates" pacing their streets', but as a smaller town they 'were experiencing only the overflowings [*sic*] of the pollution'.[5] They realised that numbers had increased greatly and that there existed 'an agency for the immigration and training of prostitutes as complete as any which have shocked us in the record of metropolitan crime'. They explained that girls were 'decoyed' from their family homes in more rural locations and taken to Blackburn, and that even 'foreign girls' (from outside the British Isles) were turning up too.[6]

By the 1860s there were a growing number of decoyed women identified, as the widening horror of the system of sexual exploitation was revealed to the public amid the frenzied horrors of national prostitution concerns. In 1863 a young dancer was decoyed from London to a music hall in Burnley. She had been persuaded to travel up to Burnley because 'the terms were very good', and the establishment seemed respectable.[7] But shortly after, her mother Jane Ball received information that 'the house was of a disreputable character and that the owner decoyed girls there from all parts for the purpose of prostitution'. Mrs Ball had been contacted by a member of a temperance society who had rescued her daughter but didn't have the funds to return her. Without the funds herself, she therefore applied to Southwark magistrate for money to send to the society. She was given the money, which she sent up to Burnley. Temperance societies were working across the country to help girls who had been pulled into prostitution, along with societies to protect fallen women and the police.

Traffic from Peterborough to Stamford

The movement of sex workers wasn't always a large-scale cross-border affair; more often than not it was invisible outside the walls of the brothel, only being revealed during a much larger criminal case. One of the Life Stories focuses on Susan and Mary Ann Tingey, who were originally from Eye, near Peterborough. They found their names in the paper in 1860 due to the murder of a wealthy Stamford resident, Elizabeth Pulley, by her neighbour Henry Corby. Miss Pulley was originally thought to have died by spontaneous combustion alone in her Stamford St Martin's townhouse, but her death was later revealed as a cunning and brutal murder by a man she knew.[8] As the charge of murder was placed on Corby, a large investigation set out to determine his movements on the days around her death. That was when a case of coerced prostitute migration was discovered.

Susan and Mary Ann had been living in Peterborough Workhouse. Older sister Mary Ann left to work at the Slaters Arms in St Leonard's Street in Peterborough under the pretence of working as a servant, but in reality, she was working as a prostitute. Mary Ann's brothel keeper, Mary Ann Smith, was friends with 'Mother Hainsworth', a brothel keeper in Stamford, around 13 miles away. That's where Susan ended up when she left the workhouse, being taken from Peterborough to work for Mother Hainsworth at the Marquis of Granby on the High Street in Stamford St Martin's.

Susan was one of several prostitutes kept at The Marquis, and we know all of the prostitutes in both brothels were victims of debt bondage, which is a form of entrapment or slavery. The women would have been told they owed their brothel keepers considerable sums of money – debt – for anything from their lodgings, food, drink, laundry, dresses, and even their travel costs to move them to the brothel. Susan, along with Caroline Bolton and Ellen Houchen, found herself trapped in the Marquis of Granby which was run by Mr and Mrs Hainsworth. The inn was 'most eligibly situated in the best part of St Martin's' on the Great North Road and had been run by the Hainsworths since at least 1853.[9] The police knew it was the scene of all manner of dreadful deeds describing it as 'a "den of iniquity"', but were powerless to act until the Henry Corby case blew open the proverbial doors of The Marquis.[10] A short case followed the Pulley-Corby murder trial when the Hainsworths found themselves in the dock. The voices of the prostitutes were damning, and revealed how poorly they were treated. The inn was described as being 'a veritable pandemonium, where young lads of tender age were encouraged to congregate, smoke, drink and revel, amid the coarse jests of the abandoned fallen ones who were harboured there'.[11]

The article explained that it wasn't until Susan gave a statement for the Henry Corby case that the police knew the full extent of the conditions the women were kept in, and had the ability to charge the Hainsworths. Susan, Caroline and Ellen gave their evidence in front of the local magistrates and much of it was, of course, unfit for publication. Their evidence 'disclosed a systematic course of the most disgusting immorality and debasement', and revealed that 'they were glad to escape from the clutches of the woman who kept guard over them'.

Ellen Houchen's story was the most tragic. She had been living in Peterborough when Mrs Hainsworth procured her; she had travelled to Peterborough deliberately to procure Ellen and tried more than once to do so. Ellen had remined for a while at The Marquis, but had left by the time of the Corby case because 'her visitors fell off', meaning she was not bringing in any money for Mrs Hainsworth. This was common in brothels where young women who had taken to drink or bad temper found themselves rejected by first the men and then by their keepers. Ellen and all the other girls, had to pay Mrs Hainsworth 2s per week for their lodgings, so Ellen was in debt at the time Mrs Hainsworth let her go. Therefore, Mrs Hainsworth took Ellen's dresses as payment for her debt, before kicking her out onto the streets of Stamford Baron. Without a penny to her name, a friend in sight, or any more to wear than her underwear, she had no choice but to present herself to the nearest workhouse on Barnack Road.

We can presume that Susan was also procured from Peterborough in a very similar method by Mrs Hainsworth along with Caroline, who was also said to be from Peterborough. We know from the workhouse and court records that Susan could not have been at The Marquis for long because she was in gaol for the whole of January of that year after absconding from the workhouse in workhouse clothing, which was classed as theft. The absolute maximum time she would have spent at The Marquis was three months, but it is more likely to be closer to two, allowing for the time taken to procure Susan and persuade her to go to The Marquis.

After the case, Susan went on to have an extraordinary life, following her sister to London (See their Life Story). Mr Hainsworth (as man of the house) was fined £5 17s 6d, which is barely half of the total fine they could have received. They were warned that if it happened again they would receive the full £10 fine. They moved on, becoming tenants of The Talbot in Stamford, continuing to run a disreputable house, but in a more secluded location. Henry Corby, the man who set the ball in motion that led to the girls' escape, hanged himself in Stamford Gaol.

Continental Women

Women and girls from the Continent were being moved around in significant numbers during the Victorian period, in particular those from Germany and France, and later Belgium. Migrants from Germany were the second largest group arriving in England after the Irish and could be found right across the country. Many women and girls worked as musicians and servants, but others were not so fortunate. In 1846 an account was relayed of a group of German girls observed at Woburn, Bedfordshire by two men. There was one woman in charge of twenty girls, and they were walking to Manchester. The woman claimed to have been working in a mill in Manchester and had been asked by the mill owner to go to Germany to bring back more workers. They were to be paid 2d a day and provided with lodgings, but the men knew this was not enough money for their work and were very suspicious that the 'luckless wretches' would 'inevitably become the victims of prostitution, disease and untimely death'.[12]

The trade from France was very well organised, with young girls 'bought and sold in France and imported into this country like any other commodity'.[13] An 1854 court case brought by Margaret Reginbal against Germain Marmaysee, her 'importer', revealed details of how she had come to England. Margaret had lived in Havre-de-Grace and been sent to England on 27 December 1853; she believed she was going to be working as a perfumer. By the time she realised the type of house she had been taken to, she was already in a large amount of debt to Germain and didn't know anybody in London who could help her. She said that the girls kept in the house were not allowed out without company, which explains why so few were identified around the country; they were kept inside brothels by their importers and it was only exceptional cases like these that exposed the traffic in foreign girls.

In 1854 there was a case of a single girl being abducted from Germany and taken to Hull, but she was one of many such girls. Auguste Heinroth was 17 and had been working in a bar in Altona, Germany, when Christian Shauntoff, a Danish sailor, set his sights on her. He visited the bar often and spent some time persuading the girl to join him and his wife in England as a servant at the inn they were going to run, promising her much more money than she was earning. She joined the couple on their voyage to Hull, but after a few days in the town Shauntoff declared he had no money and she would have to 'go on to the streets or starve'.[14] Despite Auguste's protests, Mrs Shauntoff enticed a man off the street and plied Auguste with drink so that she would participate in 'her ruin'. The couple continued to threaten and abuse her, and when she attempted to flee back to Germany they took her clothes from her, so she was forced to remain under their roof. After a trial at the Hull Michaelmas Quarter Sessions, Christian was found guilty of five charges and sentenced to two years in gaol with hard labour. The following day he was tried for assaulting Auguste and sentenced to an additional six months in gaol, this time without hard labour.[15] The story reached the national press, with a London paper claiming: 'There is an immense number of German prostitutes in Hull and it is stated that a that a regular trade has been carried on in the bringing of them over.'[16] Auguste's story was, again, just the tip of the iceberg.

The contents of a letter regarding the trade of European women were retold in a newspaper in 1856. The letter claimed that there was a trade in women to and from Germany, specifically Hamburg, which was the centre of prostitution in Germany.[17] The letter made no reference to London, but to the trade of women to and from Liverpool facilitated by one unnamed woman. The correspondent claimed that the woman would head out to Germany with a group of young English girls aged around 15 or 16 and leave them there, bringing back a similar contingency of German girls.

We might expect the girls to travel in and out of Liverpool because it was a major port, but to sail from Liverpool, on the west coast of England, over to Germany in the east would be a lengthy and tiresome journey. The girls were instead moved in and out of Hull, affording a considerably shorter journey by boat. Inbound girls were sent on from Hull to Liverpool and Manchester, and outbound girls continued on to Hamburg where, after remaining for a couple of years, went on to other towns and cities in Germany.

A report from 1864 claims that there was an organised network running small groups of girls from Germany into Rotterdam in the Netherlands, a major port. The girls were 'between the ages of 15 and 20', and 'unaccompanied by either parents or any members of their family, but accompanied by a woman named Brehm, whose husband keeps a public-house of bad repute in Rotterdam'.[18] The girls sailed to England with Mrs Brehm and then on to their final destination. They may have been able to slip past authorities in England and Rotterdam, but the Prussian authorities were aware and were determined to stop the trade.

The trade in Dutch and Belgian girls was less visible in the middle of the century, but on the subject of 'The Great Social Evil', it was suggested in *The Times* that 'some restraint were placed on the introduction of young girls from Hamburg, Belgium, France, &c', suggesting that there was still concern in the traffic of women from Belgium.[19] The majority of these imported women lived in London, where there had been 'a very large number of foreign prostitutes recently imported' in the mid-1850s.[20] These included the likes of Eleanor Posselman, 'a native of Holland', who was a nuisance on the streets with English prostitutes in 1856, and Alice Leroy who had been abducted from Belgium in 1854 under the false belief she was going to learn millinery skills in London. Belgian girls didn't just end up in London, but were also sent to other migrant hotspots including Liverpool, where Madame Annie Rosenberg arrived in 1857 with 'three young Belgian girls' destined for a brothel[21]. She was 'bound over' for the sum of £400 (equivalent to over £40,000 today).

The traffic of young girls for sex work from the Continent was bidirectional, with English girls sent over the Channel under the guidance of women such as Baroness de Steinberg in 1862. She was accused of 'decoying good looking English girls', and sending them 'to the chief Continental cities, where they [were] caged in brothels and compelled to prostitute themselves'.[22] A £125 reward was on offer for her capture.

It was the trading of young English girls to Belgium that was at the centre of a scandal known as 'The Maiden Tribute of Modern Babylon' in 1885, over two decades after the Baroness de Steinberg story. The editor of the *Pall Mall Gazette*, W.T. Stead, released a series of articles exposing the 'White Slave Trade' of young women – virgins – being sent to the Continent.[23] It was a series of explosive revelations detailing the ease of purchasing a virgin – specifically 13-year-old Eliza Armstrong – and the sophisticated networks that operated to ship these women to brothels on the Continent. It was a pivotal moment in the history of child sexual exploitation, undercover journalism and human traffic, and led to the raising of the age of consent from 13 to 16 in the Criminal Law Amendment Act of the same year.

What led to W.T. Stead's undercover journalism was communication from Benjamin Scott, Chamberlain of London, and Bramwell Booth, the Chief of Staff of the Salvation Army. Booth and his organisation were walking the streets of London and were aware of the extent of the traffic in women and the harm that was being caused to girls as young as 13 (the legal age of consent).

The Salvation Army was one of many societies trying to identify and find a solution for the huge numbers of young prostitutes in the country at the time. They knew how deplorable the situation was and that London was the centre of the worst forms of depravity.

The legacy of the exposé was the Criminal Law Amendment Act, which aimed to protect young girls from being exploited, and a range of other new acts that aimed to punish procurers and brothel keepers instead of prostitutes. It also led the Dutch government to reach out a hand to their neighbours and offer a treaty that encouraged them to work together 'for the mutual prevention of the traffic in girls'.[24]

The exploitation of migrant girls and women for sexual purposes was a considerable issue in the Victorian period both within England and across country borders. The full extent of the number of girls decoyed into the trade will never fully be realised, but through the few examples we have, we can at least know what they experienced and be thankful that some were saved. We can also be thankful that the deeds and voices of a few people were able to highlight this trade nationally and to start to minimise its impact.

Life Story: The Tingey Sisters

There are many erroneous assumptions made about the lives of Victorian prostitutes. By following the lives of Susan and Mary Ann Tingey, we can consider that the label of a prostitute may be nothing but a snapshot of an exploited woman. Conversely, that once labelled a prostitute and exposed to the life, the desire to flirt, enjoy illicit sex, and entertain, was hard-wired into the mind of the fallen woman. The comparison of two sisters allows us to consider two women with almost identical childhoods and what their lives looked like before and after they were labelled.

The Tingey sisters were born in Eye, near Peterborough, to Elijah and Ann Tingey. Their brother George was born first, followed by Mary Ann in 1842, Susan in 1844, and later by little brother William in 1847. There was a large age gap between their parents – twelve years – with Ann marrying at 18 and giving birth to George a year later. Little is known about Elijah or Ann, but Elijah did appear in front of the magistrates in 1850 accused of 'cruelty to a horse at Peterboro'', for which he was fined (and paid) £2 with £1 costs.[25]

Census records indicate that they were living in the hamlet of Eye Green in 1851, which is a tiny offshoot of the main village of Eye, but ten years earlier, at the time of the 1841 census, they had been in 'Eye Town'. The change of residence was on account of the death of both Mary Tingey, Elijah's mother who lived with, or next to, the family, and Ann, his wife. Elijah was an agricultural labourer, which was common for the rural setting.

Eye Green was a scattered hamlet of farm buildings and small terraces houses for agricultural workers. The children all went to school in Eye and would have walked past the corn mill and cemetery before arriving at their school. They would have walked past the new church of St Matthew and watched it being built, replacing the earlier medieval church. Sadly, they did not live there long enough to see the spire erected onto the tower ten years later, or the arrival of the railway. William was one of the first children baptised in St Matthew's in June, only two months after the building was completed. A year later, on 2 February 1848, it was also the site of the funeral for their mother Ann, who died at the age of 30. George was 8 or 9, Mary Ann 5, Susan 3 and William less than 9 months. The 1851 census shows them living together in Eye Green with a domestic servant, a widow aged 35 named Mary Padmore, who was hired to replace their work of their mother.

What is desperately sad is that three years after the census, the family were living in Peterborough Workhouse. They had gone from living as a small rural family unit to grieving and destitute in a few short years. We do not have evidence that the entire family had entered the workhouse – it is possible that little William, who was only 6 or 7, was taken in by a relative – but there is clear evidence that Elijah, George and Susan were there, and we can confidently assume that Mary Ann was there too. George appeared in the Union Punishment book on 14 February 1854 when he would have been 14 or 15. Just over a year later, his father was dead. Elijah Tingey, aged only 48, died in Peterborough Workhouse and was returned to Eye to be buried there on 24 March. This suggests his plot had been paid for at the same time as Ann's, which is why he avoided a pauper's grave in Peterborough.

At the ages of 16, 12, 10 and 7, the Tingey children were orphans and at least two were in the workhouse – their outlooks would have seemed bleak, particularly for the younger children. George was an adult, so he would have been able to find work and escape from the workhouse; the girls and William, however, would have to remain until they found a way out. Susan thought she'd found a way out in 1859, at the age of 15. She'd scaled the union wall and escaped with her friends, Jane Baxter and Jane Preston. However, in escaping in the union clothing, they were guilty of theft. Susan and Jane Baxter were sentenced to one month of hard labour in gaol, with Jane Preston given two weeks.

Susan had escaped only a few days after her brother George had married in Raunds. He married on Boxing Day and, knowing he was literate, it is possible that he had written to his siblings to inform them of this, potentially offering them a home with him and his new bride. It is possible that Susan had escaped to attempt to reach George, or had attempted to get to him before his wedding, but she didn't make it and, after being sentenced on 31 December, she spent the first month of 1860 in Peterborough Gaol, which was only metres from the workhouse (see map on page x). It was a particularly inauspicious start to Susan's year, a year that would find her name and Mary Ann's, plastered across newspapers across the country.

Susan would likely have returned to the workhouse at the beginning of February, but neither she nor Mary Ann were there for long. By March, both sisters were living in public houses, Mary Ann at The Slaters Arms in St Leonard's Street near Peterborough North Station, and Susan at The Marquis of Granby on High Street, St Martin's in Stamford Baron. We know this because the sisters were both working as prostitutes and both were caught up in the case of Henry Corby, the Stamford man who had robbed and killed his elderly neighbour and enjoyed a spree with prostitutes before he was arrested and ended his life (see pages 114–17).

Susan was only 15 at the time of the Corby case. It was neither illegal for her to be a prostitute, nor for her to be having sex – the legal age of consent was 13 and would not rise to 16 until 1885 (see pages 93–4). Susan had been 'procured', and kept in a form of debt bondage in the Marquis of Granby, under the watchful eye of her keepers.

In contrast, Mary Ann was still living in Peterborough and had some sort of relationship or association with Henry Corby. He deliberately travelled to Peterborough to ask Mary Ann to run away to London with him after the murder. This also tells us he either found her attractive, or felt he could earn money from her on the streets of London.

We also know from the court case that the sisters were close. Instead of going to London with Henry, Mary Ann persuaded him to take her to Stamford to see Susan. In what might have been an attempt to impress Mary Ann, Henry gifted Susan with a pair of boots that he claimed had been bought for his wife (he'd stolen them from Miss Pulley, the woman he murdered), and 2s 6d to spend at the fair in Stamford.

Thankfully, both girls escaped their situation and moved away from the scene of the incident. Miss Pulley's murder did at least allow several vulnerable girls to be rescued from their keepers.

By the 1861 census a year later, Susan was back in Peterborough and lodging at 3 Bruff's Row on Eastfield Road, near to notorious Burton's Row and on the junction with Prince's Gardens. Susan's occupation was given as a lace maker, which is one of the lowest type of work available and was often synonymous with prostitution. Given her past behaviour, her position close to Burton's Row, which was home to prostitutes, and the fact there weren't any other lace makers, it is likely she was working at least partly as a prostitute.

Although Mary Ann did not appear in Peterborough in the census, she may well have been living there too. She was in London at the time, visiting a George Sculthorpe at 26 Manning Street in Marylebone, with 4-year-old Lizzie Sculthorpe. George and Lizzie were both identified as being from Peterborough, and George was working as a labourer and living above a milk shop.

On 17 November 1861, George and Mary Ann married at Christchurch in Marylebone. They both signed the marriage register but their witnesses, John and Sarah Griffin, both left a shaky mark. The marriage record tells us George was working as an excavator and his father, Robert Sculthorpe, was a labourer. Mary Ann's father was identified as Elijah Tingey and she described him as a horse dealer, which is the only time that employment is attributed to him. Perhaps in death, she could claim he was whatever she wished, or there was a period where he worked as a horse dealer before he entered Peterborough Workhouse.

Their eldest child, Eliza Ann, was born in Peterborough and was christened at St John's on 23 March 1862. We can be absolutely certain that Mary Ann was pregnant at the time of her wedding and may well have been heavily pregnant. Several other children followed, but they were all born in London, where George was working as an excavator and so would have been earning more money than a general labourer. It was likely he was involved in excavating the underground; the first line opened in 1863 and was between Paddington and Farringdon via King's Cross, so George was in a perfect location. By 1871 he had moved the family to Kirkleatham in Yorkshire, where he and his childhood friend John were working as ironstone miners. By this point they had four children: two girls and two boys, with the three London-born children born in different London boroughs suggesting that they moved house to follow the extension of the underground railway lines and to get the best work possible.

Any association that Mary Ann had with prostitution was long gone. Her identification in the Henry Corby scandal was brief, and she was married and expecting a child less than two years later. Her husband George earned a good wage and their move to London benefited them both. Staying in Peterborough would not have given them the same possibilities and her reputation as a prostitute from the workhouse may well have followed her, as it did her sister Susan, who had remained in the city.

Susan appeared in three court cases in 1863. In April she fought with two other 'nymphs of the pavé', for which she was fined.[26] In July she fought another prostitute with Mary Ann, with both sisters receiving fines and in the November, she caused the courts quite the dilemma after selling all of her boyfriend's furniture while he was out, before running off. This was potentially the money she needed to leave Peterborough and move to London, which is where she next appeared – but her life was about to look very different.

On Boxing Day 1869, Susan married Alfred Peck Stevens by licence at St Stephen's Church in Hammersmith. He was a widower and the son of a gentleman, and lived near Regents Park; she claimed her father Elijah had been a farmer and she lived in Shepherd's Bush at the time. Nothing seems remarkable until we learn that Alfred Peck Stevens was also known as 'The Great Vance', and was a famous music hall performer (see a poster of him on page X). It would be an absolute cliché to suggest that Susan moved to London in the hope of finding work and was reduced to picking up men in the theatres and music halls, as countless women had done before her, but she hadn't. Susan was also a music hall singer.[27] Once married, Susan, or Emma as she was often known, continued to work alongside her husband on the stage, performing around the country.

They remained together for less than five years before separating, in 1874; Susan continued to work as a singer under the name Emma Vance. A clue in the *Kentish Gazette* reveals why their marriage failed. It stated that Alfred had taken out a summons against Emma for assaulting him, but neither turned up in court to make their case, so it was dropped.[28] She had been fined for fighting with prostitutes in Peterborough, so his accusation of assault does sound plausible.

In an unexpected turn Susan filed for a restitution of conjugal rights in 1883, thirteen years after marrying Alfred and nine years after they had separated. She gave her address as 60 Wynford Road, St Pancras, and stated that she had lived with Alfred in a variety of places until 1874, but that there had been no children born, which was not unusual for a former prostitute. In Susan's request for restitution, she claimed Alfred had kicked her out of their home on 24 July (after the summons) and had refused to have anything to do with her after that, but for no good reason. But her husband responded to the accusation in April with his own fire. He was quite detailed in his accusations of adultery, claiming firstly that they agreed to separate and that she:

- Committed adultery with an unknown man on 28th and 29th July 1875 at the Queens Hotel in Hastings.
- Committed adultery frequently with Sir Capel Fitzgerald.
- Committed adultery with Oswald Braine in Margate in August 1881 and countless other occasions. (He was another Music Hall performer.)
- Committed adultery with many other men.

These are quite precise charges and we can either assume that they still had shared friends, he had been following her movements, or she was boastful in her conquests.

Sir Capel Fitzgerald is a shortened form of Sir Joseph Capel Judkin-Fitzgerald, 4th Baronet (Co. Tipperary). He was not a fine example of the landed gentry and had a penchant for gambling, sex and reprehensible behaviour. In 1878, years after his downward spiral had begun, he travelled to Paris with Susan to see the Paris Exhibition. While there they could have been lucky enough to see the head of the Statue of Liberty, Alexander Graham Bell and his telephone, or maybe a typewriter. Their trip was not the success that Susan had hoped it would be, and on their return she accused him of stealing a quantity of jewellery from her during the trip.

The case revealed she lived at 36 Westbourne Park Villas, a very nice house in a respectable area. The value of the jewellery, which included a lot of diamonds, came to around £400, which is incredible given that she was a penniless orphan at the age of 10. Susan, it appears, had been living there under the 'protection of a gentleman' for two years – in other words, she was living as a mistress of a very wealthy man.[29] We can assume that the jewellery was given to her by the man or was lent to her as part of the arrangement. Let us not forget that she was still married at this point and this arrangement does not appear in her husband's evidence against her. Her evidence at the trial also reveals that she first met Fitzgerald in 1875, before his financial situation worsened and before she had started living under the protection of a gentleman. Their relationship had only restarted six weeks before their Paris trip; it wouldn't be a wild jump to suggest that all of his other friends had disowned him following his descent into bankruptcy, and he saw Susan as both a source of fun and income.

Despite the considerable evidence against Fitzgerald, including testimony from a policeman who had found him booked into a hotel under a false name – and his own admission that he had taken her jewellery, he was found not guilty. His lawyer claimed because the event occurred in France, it could not be tried in England (and he had been held in prison awaiting trial too). The word of a high-class mistress was almost inadmissible against a baronet, even if he had been declared bankrupt and behaved horrendously; her moral crimes were far greater than his crimes would ever be in the eyes of the law – and of a jury.

A few hints of her looks, personality and relationship come through in the court testimonies, which add colour to her life. A description in the *Illustrated Police News* states she was: 'round featured, pale, inclined to be stout, wearing a blue close-fitting dress, with hat and feather. In the witness box she maintained a great deal of composure.'[30] It also featured an image of Sir Capel on the front page. From letters produced we know Fitzgerald called her Emmie, reminding us that she was using the name Emma at that point in her life. He also called her 'my darling', suggesting a great deal of intimacy or fondness between them. We know she had a variety of pieces of jewellery including 'diamond stars' earrings, three diamond ring, bracelets, necklaces etc., and that she liked to travel around by cab. She also stated that she had dined regularly at the glamorous Café Royale, which is now known as the Hotel Café Royale and was a regular haunt by figures such as Oscar Wilde and George Bernard Shaw in following years.

Amazingly, Fitzgerald appears to have returned to his wife after this event, for she gave birth to their third child, a daughter, about a year later in 1879. But they did not remain together, his wife Constance moved to the Channel Islands, where she remained. He returned to Ireland, where he died in 1917; both his heirs predeceased him, and so the baronetcy died with him.

We can imagine that this case would not have been taken kindly by the gentleman who had been furnishing her lifestyle, hence the suggestion of further lovers by her ex-husband. The best assumption we can make is that by 1883 she had exhausted all of her money and options, which is why she asked the court to have her status as a wife reinstated. Her plea was unsuccessful.

In 1885 Susan appeared in the papers again, twice. She had been living with Oswald Braine near Regent's Park; they had been harassing Alfred at events 'and annoyed him in every possible manner'.[31] This had resulted in a number of claims being made in the papers, started by Alfred's pseudo-wife Eunice, claiming that Susan was not associated with them. Alfred published an article in *The Telegraph* stating that they 'were in no way related'.[32] He claimed they had not married and that 'Emma Vance' was not his wife. This had incensed her and was the catalyst for her lover Oswald punching Alfred in the jaw and 'knocking him off his seat' at the Trocadero Music Hall. Oswald was bound over for £500 for the next six months and charged five guineas costs. She attempted to bring a libel case against Alfred in the following year, but the courts stated she could not prosecute him on libel charges because they were married, so the case was dropped.

Alfred died from heart disease on the anniversary of his and Susan's wedding in 1888. He had been taken ill on stage in Knightsbridge and was declared dead by the time he reached the hospital. If it hadn't been confirmed by his doctor that he was already very ill from heart disease, this would have looked very suspicious indeed.

By the 1891 census Susan was using the name Emma officially and living in Tavistock Chambers by St George's Church on Museum Street,

Bloomsbury, a prime location. She had one female servant and was living independently. Tavistock Chambers was only 3 years old and we may question how she was able to afford such an impressive location if she wasn't still living as someone's mistress. The search for the final years of her life is still underway.

Mary Ann and George spent their final years living with their daughter Susan, her husband John Carter (a railway tunnel miner) and their grandchildren. George died in 1906 shortly before John's brother Robert; both shared a plot and headstone in Margravine Cemetery, Hammersmith. By the 1911 census John had become the landlord of the Red Lion on St Ann's Road, Notting Hill, and was sharing his home with Mary Ann, his daughters and granddaughters, meaning that there were four generations living together. Mary Ann died in 1912 at the age of 70, joining the others in the family plot and on the headstone; her daughter Susan joined her the following year.

Mary Ann's life is proof that prostitutes could successfully marry and live long, comfortable lives with their husband and children. Had she remained in Peterborough, her reputation and life experiences would have remained with her and her husband, but moving down to London allowed them the anonymity to start again with a clean slate. We know when she visited Susan in Peterborough she was drawn into a fight, but there was no evidence of that in London, even when Susan moved there too. Mary Ann lived a long life surrounded by loving family and was mourned on her death. Flowers can still be left at her grave by her descendants, which is a luxury denied to many women who lived as prostitutes.

Susan's life was incredible. From a small hamlet she travelled to Peterborough Workhouse where she was orphaned. From there she visited gaol and then found herself trapped in a brothel. After a couple of unsuccessful years in Peterborough she moved to London and became a music hall singer. Her marriage to 'The Great Vance' elevated her status with other entertainers and she continued to sing after her separation from Alfred. She enjoyed the protection of rich men, living her life as a high-class mistress, but Susan also enjoyed fame and attention, and dragged her husband through the courts on libel accounts and an implausible challenge to gain restitution to her marriage bed. She changed her name, making her very difficult to find in the records, but we do at least know she lived in comfort in the very respectable area of Bloomsbury in London. For a girl who was probably given up on in the workhouse, she did alright for herself.

Chapter 10

Go, Sin No More: Life After Prostitution

Prostitution, for the vast majority of women, was a temporary state made necessary by destitution, or a label they had acquired after behaving in a disorderly, unfeminine, or immoral manner. Even for those who were prostitutes for many years, there came a point at which they would struggle to earn a living from such a precarious trade and be forced to leave the profession.

For some girls and young women, it was a stage in their life between childhood and marriage, for others it represented a few weeks or months until they found a better situation and for some, being labelled as a prostitute was little more than a traumatic event that captured them at their lowest point in the legal system. An example of this temporary state came from London in 1841, where several poor girls were procured, kept locked in a brothel for a couple of months, and then released again, no longer of use to the keeper. The conclusion in one of the newspapers was that the girls would either be able to 'return to their parents [and] endeavour to hide the defilement which they ha[d] suffered', or 'they [could] give themselves up for lost and continue the course into which they ha[d] been entrapped'.[1] The girls that returned to their parents would never have been labelled prostitutes because they were never seen outside of the brothel, but those who 'continued the course' may well have appeared in the records, longing to escape but not knowing how to.

There were, however, several routes out of prostitution. The main ones being:

- Marriage or cohabiting
- Employment
- A reformatory, refuge, or home for fallen women
- Workhouse, Prison, or transportation
- Disease and death

The route out was, for many, not a straight line, but more of a sine wave. The women would find an escape (e.g., a man or a job) and that would fail, forcing them back into prostitution, or they would enter the workhouse or reformatory in the hope of leading a more moral life, only to be lured back by persistent friends. The route to reform was very austere and one that many prostitutes failed to follow to a successful end. The path into marriage, however, was one that potentially offered the best outcome and was encouraged from every level of society.

Marriage and Cohabiting

The Victorians believed in the sanctity of marriage and that a woman was only truly respectable if she was married. This was based on Christian doctrines, often included in letters to newspapers that were echoed in the pulpit. 'Go, sin no more', was one of many pieces of advice to prostitutes in 1850 when the Committee for the Protection of Young Females and for the Prevention of Prostitution was building up support in the newspapers, along with the reminder that 'Marriage is honourable in all.'[2] Plenty of prostitutes married and went on to live quieter lives with no hint of their past, as was the case for Mary Ann Tingey and Emma Browning (See Chapter 1). It was the same situation for Elizabeth Harrison until she brought a rape charge against her family doctor (see Chapter 3). The family unit in which the man worked and the woman tended to the house and children was the prescribed route to a successful life. Many marriages failed, however, and women found themselves destitute.

It was almost impossible for the lower classes to divorce due to its cost and complexity, so one option for abandoned women was to cohabit with a new lover. They lived as husband and wife, sometimes declaring that they were married, despite the lack of a marriage record to prove it. On census records the women labelled themselves as the man's 'housekeeper' rather than wife, with the married status of one or both of the couple giving the clue to their true relationship. This cohabiting status allowed people to live together without being arrested for bigamy, but also allowed them to move on should that relationship fail. There were plenty of accounts of cohabiting prostitutes, so it wasn't always a route out of prostitution, but it could be a precursor to marriage following the death of a spouse, or in the case of Catherine Thirkettle and Eliza, the sister of Martha Baines (see their Life Stories), until she could persuade him to marry her.

The relationship of Fred King and Emily Skellet in Stamford serves to remind us that these relationships could be very loving. Emily had been born in Ketton, Rutland, in 1830 and baptised in 1838. Her start in life had not been great and she and her sisters Sarah Ann and Fanny found themselves in need of assistance at the workhouse in 1850. Three years later Emily had married Samuel Holland, but their marriage was not successful and by the 1861 census she was living apart from her husband and had taken a lodger, Jane Baudice. She was said to be working as a 'sempstress', like many women on her street, but she was also known as a prostitute. By the following year she had started cohabiting with Fred King, a musician and son of Susan Plowright, later Cummings (see Chapter 4). Fred and Emily ran the Musicians Arms beerhouse together and, despite constant fighting with Fred's family and their musicians, they had a tight and loving bond.

Tragically, Fred died in 1870, but he had earned enough money from his beerhouse (or illegal behaviour) to be able to provide for Emily and his mother Susan after his death. He knew he was going to die after being diagnosed with an abscess in his stomach and swelling in his brain, and had taken excellent legal advice.[3] On his death he left money to Emily and some furniture to Susan, but he did so in the knowledge that the items he had bequeathed to them would remain their property and couldn't be taken by their husbands because the Women's Property Act had been introduced only days before he passed away. It may be difficult to find examples of love and care in the prostitute records, but this shows that Emily was loved and that cohabiting could be successful, even if this tale ended in tragedy.

Elizabeth Thurlow's relationship with her husband did not get off to the best start. She had been born in Woodbridge, Suffolk in December 1851, and moved to nearby Ipswich as her widowed mother struggled to keep her. By the age of 17 she was working as a prostitute in a pub by the dock and, following a couple of wild years, ended up in St Matthew's Industrial Home for Girls in Ipswich- a reformatory.[4] After leaving the school in 1871, she returned home to support her mother and younger siblings and put the skills she had learnt in the reformatory to good use. On a night out only a few months later, she was assaulted by Frederick Copeman in a pub in the middle of Woodbridge, for which he received a week in gaol.[5] During the next five years their relationship changed from that of enemies to lovers and Fred and Elizabeth married, aged 25 and 24 respectively. As we might suspect, it was not the easiest of marriages, with Fred getting into several fights with other people in the following years. The couple weren't fortunate enough to have children of their own, but they did raise several of Elizabeth's nephews and nieces and had a good relationship with them. Elizabeth and Fred's marriage lasted forty-five years until Fred's death in 1921, and for the final years of her life, Elizabeth lived with the nephew she had raised as a son. She died in 1942, aged 91, proof that prostitutes could go on to live long and loving lives.

Employment, Reformatories, Refuges and Homes

The natural progression for a successful prostitute with good relationships and a number of clients was to run a brothel and/or work procuring young girls for themselves and other people. These could both be carried out while the woman was still working as a prostitute, as we saw with Esther Smith in Chapter 1, and Mary Ann Griffiths in Chapter 9, so the change of status from prostitute to brothel keeper was often subtle. There were also plenty of former prostitutes who ran drinking establishments and lodging houses, using their businesses to support and exploit other prostitutes and continue the cycle. They were businesswomen making the most of opportunities when they came their way, just as they had when they'd been working as a prostitute.

Respectable employment was a preferred route out of prostitution for institutions supporting prostitutes and many of the women themselves. Enabling the women to provide for themselves through regular, honest and respectable work meant that they weren't reliant on a friendly landlord, or good weather to meet men in the street, and they weren't fearful of catching a disease.

Employment was the ultimate goal for girls who ended up in the reformatories, penitentiaries and homes for fallen women. The aim was to reform them and teach them useful, employable skills such as sewing and domestic duties, as well as the three Rs. The story of Elizabeth Thurlow, above, shows that it did work for some women, who then went on to live long, respectable lives.

A common issue for penitent homes was a lack of money or a lack of room. In Portsmouth in 1870, the Home and Refuge at Landport for the Reception of Fallen Women made a desperate appeal for more money to enlarge their building.[6] The home already had more than double the women it was designed for and there many more who were 'sincerely anxious to quit the servitude of prostitution'. This was during the CD Acts and Portsmouth was one of the targeted locations, so the sincere desire to leave the profession was likely to have been accelerated by the restrictions and the possibility of 'obtaining situations' or being returned to their friends.

However, the *Nuneaton Observer* noted in 1893 that 'in most towns [...] there have been established homes for fallen women which have met with but little success'.[7] This failure of the homes was described elsewhere as an apathy towards helping the fallen, but in reality, it was apathy or disinterest by men.

This apathy was seen at a meeting in North Shields to discuss opening a 'Home for Friendless and Fallen Women' in Tynemouth in 1880.[8] A few dignitaries were present, as were 'a number of ladies', but the quantity of men in attendance was described as 'very shy'. The article revealed that a Miss Bamford had been leading the way in offering support for fallen women and that in 1868 she had organised a 'midnight coffee supper' to encourage 'fallen girls to forsake their ways'. She had space for three girls to be helped, but seven or eight stayed after the midnight coffee to ask for help. Miss Bamford was one of a growing number of middle-class women across the country who felt it their duty or purpose to help fallen women. She had been working for over a decade to provide support for fallen women in the Tynemouth area and had changed many lives for the better.

There were some men involved in the area including the mayor, who gave up his house to accommodate the girls for a short while. But the plan was not universally accepted and there were some people who attempted to hinder its success. When friends of the fallen girls heard of their rescue, they were pretty annoyed and 'used great influence with the girls to try and get them away'. They were attempting to pull them back to the life they'd been keen to escape, possibly for the sake of friendship, but more likely for the sake of the money that could be earned from them.

Oxford's Home for Friendless Girls also had an all-female committee. They took a different approach to the problem of prostitution and rescued young girls who were without support and at risk of becoming prostitutes, working to actively steer them away from 'dangerous temptations' by providing short term accommodation and training.[9] They too were struggling with their finances and wrote a letter to the *Oxford Chronicle and Reading Gazette* begging for more subscribers. One of the subscribers was the local Board of Guardians, who was still subscribing £10 a year in 1891, two years after their plea, so we know their letter was successful.[10]

Details of a temporary home in North Shields that had operated in the late 1870s revealed the destination of thirty-seven girls:

Six were in permanent homes, nine were restored to relatives, eleven were in service, four were in various workhouses, one had been assisted to emigrate and was in service in Canada, one was in the Infirmary, four had gone back to their old life and one was lost sight of.[11]

Given that the North Shields home was temporary, the committee were hopeful that with a permanent home in Tynemouth, they could help more women in the area and provide them all with a better outcome. The expense of buying property and the running of the home was considerable, but was assisted by money raised by the women who had organised a committee and gathered funds. The home did open, but only lasted a few years; the outcome of the rescued women was 'fairly satisfactory'.[12]

Emigration was something that women from Urania Cottage, the home co-founded and managed by Charles Dickens, were encouraged to do. They travelled to Australia, the US and Canada, just as the woman from North Shields had. At the Birmingham Refuge for Fallen Women they recorded 290 women passing through their doors between 1855 and 1863, and 7 of those women also emigrated, but not one of the 1,287 women who left the home in Liverpool emigrated, possibly because so many were already migrants.[13]

The long-lasting home for fallen women in Hull provided an account of the destination of all of the women who had been through their doors in the twelve years it had been open:

121 restored to their parents or relations,
93 placed out in respectable service,
3 married from the home,
1 apprenticed to a dressmaker,
4 sent to work at the factory,
34 sent to the workhouse,
81 left at their own request,
6 dismissed for improper conduct,
14 ran away,
3 sent to the Hull Penitentiary,
1 sent to York Penitentiary,
3 dismissed on account of being married,
1 taken away by the police for felony,
1 died in the Infirmary,
1 died in the home.[14]

Including the 12 women still in the home, that made a total of 379 (10 more than the paper claimed) women who had passed through their doors. The majority of the women had a positive outcome on leaving the home and it was seen as a success. These outcomes match up with the general routes out of prostitution – including three getting married and two sadly dying.

At the home in Exeter, there were again a large number of middle-class women who supported the home for fallen women. The home took in prostitutes from across Devon and had been running for fifteen years by the time of its report in 1876. It too had suffered financial issues, but the committee had worked hard to balance their books. During 1875 the home had helped a total of thirty-one girls with ten in service, one 'welcomed home by loving parents after eighteen months sojourn in the Home (the girl expressed her willingness to stay longer), four left of their own accord and four were sent away.'[15] Of the girls that went into service, many were 'highly valued' due to the training they received in the home. Those that had less impressive outcomes were claimed to have had a 'bad temper or a love of drink'.

Workhouse, Prison and Transportation

This route was not taken by choice and was not a long-term solution unless transported for life. Being gaoled meant a woman could not earn her keep by prostitution, but she was still very much labelled as one. There was a belief that women removed from their immoral brethren would repent in the austere conditions of the prison system, but this failed to acknowledge that the prison system was full of other immoral women, many of whom had been in and out of the prison gates countless times.

The same was true for the workhouse – which was so feared that women would rather earn money through prostitution than dare to enter its walls. Tales that 'children in the workhouse were killed to make pies', and that 'human body parts [were] used for workhouse dinners', kept people away for the fear that dying within its walls led to unimaginable horrors.[16] The meagre rations and cold, sparsely furnished buildings were also supposed to encourage the poor to leave and earn an honest living, not rely on support. But as the Tingey sisters' story reveals, young girls were taken from the workhouse straight into prostitution. Some of the girls from the penitent and fallen women homes entered workhouses, but there's little to suggest that a short stay there led to a positive outcome.

Transportation offered potential as the women completely escaped their previous life. Some judges stated that they hoped the time away would help them to turn their lives around; others were just glad to push the problem to another location that they didn't have to reside over. For those who died on the journey there or back, it was tantamount to a death sentence. Once transportation ended, women found themselves facing longer gaol sentences as another way to keep them off the streets.

Disease and Death

Sexual disease is often thought to be a big reason that women would be forced out of prostitution, but this wasn't the case. The CD Acts were testament to the fact that women continued to work as prostitutes when they were infected with these diseases and it was not off putting to the men who engaged with their services. In Leeds in 1840 it was believed that 80 per cent of the approximately 700 prostitutes in the city were diseased, so it was almost impossible to avoid catching, or passing on, something unpleasant. But the sex industry in Leeds was thriving and the men were not put off by the high levels of sexual disease. What was more likely to remove a prostitute from the trade was an infectious disease or illness linked to poor living conditions, drink, over-crowding, bad sanitation etc. These diseases were not something that the women necessarily lived with for long, finding themselves weakened and at the mercy of friends, family, or the workhouse. Disease was not the route out of prostitution, but ultimately a conduit to their untimely death.

Prostitute deaths in the papers included those from starvation, disease, murder, suicide, and botched abortions. Several are included elsewhere in this book, including the three women who died in fires, and 'Welsh Kit', who was murdered after leaving her lover. Poverty and the lack of a warm, dry home, food and medicine, all hastened early deaths. These were not women living in loving homes with their own bed, but women who were barely surviving at times. They were being taken to police stations in wheelbarrows because they were steaming drunk, or being refused help in hospitals because they could have infected other patients, either physically, or morally. But this is exactly why the Ladies' National Association and other organisations worked so hard to get help to the women who wanted it and to remove them from the world of prostitution – they were trying to save lives.

It is often difficult to find the exact cause of prostitute deaths, partly because of the way they were reported and partly because of the way they were investigated by coroners and doctors. Suicide and death by alcohol were the most common reasons given for a prostitute death, even if they didn't fit the situation. Even when the women died in asylums or were beaten by their husbands and lovers, the state of the liver was always considered and alcoholism was given as a contributing or primary factor. It continued the narrative that whatever state the prostitutes got into, it was their fault for drinking too much and living immorally; they were to blame for their downfall. Images like the death of Moll Hackabout in Hogarth's 'A Harlot's Progress' (see page X) did nothing but fuel this sentiment. Likewise, if a woman died after taking, or being suspected of taking, an abortifacient, then her status as a prostitute was highlighted in the report on the inquest. This happened to Mary White in Frome, Somerset in 1867, who led an 'immoral mode of life' and died from an infection after taking drugs to induce a miscarriage while six months pregnant.[17] She died in excruciating pain with 'six ounces of pus' in her pelvis and an abscess in her womb. The court case against the woman who gave her the abortifacient was abandoned.

Suicide

There endures an archetypal image of a prostitute ending her life by throwing herself into a river (usually the Thames), thanks to some famous artworks depicting their dramatic leap off a bridge (see image on page X). There certainly were plenty of prostitute drownings in rivers and docks around the country, but those who decided to end their lives didn't always follow the dramatic stereotype, nor did they always end their life by drowning. For those who did end their lives, many did so not because they had endured enough of their depraved lives (the narrative the reformers wanted us to believe), but rather for lost loves. They were distressed at yet another person letting them down, or by loss of the opportunity to escape their situation through marriage.

Looking across the country there are examples of self-administered poisoning involving oxalic acid, arsenic, strychnine and laudanum, the latter being by far the most available and common form of poisoning, whether deliberate or accidental. Sarah Ann Smith from Boston, Lincolnshire, also known as 'Grimy Smith', ended her life with 'two ounces of laudanum'.[18]

She was only 25 and had drunk an excessive amount of brandy in the hours before she asked two little girls to fetch her the laudanum. A doctor was called and attempted to pump her stomach (a very unusual event in 1877), but to no avail. She died later that day.

Elizabeth Collins (16) had been living with her two older sisters in rooms above the Hospital for Skin Diseases in Newcastle when she decided to end her life in the spring of 1889.[19] In a case of a lost love, she had gone down into the hospital in the middle of the night and taken some strychnine before returning to her lodging and writing a letter to her beloved George. She had told her older sisters what she had done but they didn't believe her until she started to feel unwell, by which time it was too late to save her. The sisters had all lived at home until six months earlier, when there had been an argument with their mother and they all fled together. Unable to support themselves they took to prostitution to pay for lodgings. Elizabeth's letter was a farewell note to 'her sweetheart' George. She was in excruciating pain before she fell into a coma and died in the early hours of the morning. Priscilla Keenleyside, the girls landlady, was charged with 'having assisted in the management of a house of ill-fame', and was sentenced to two months of hard labour.

Maria Wheeler was inconsolable at the prospect of going to prison and attempted to take her life many times while in the Bridewell in Gloucester in 1848. She had 'torn her dress and the lining from her dress and tied the shreds and lining tightly round her throat'.[20] When her dress was removed, she attempted to use her own hair, twisted round her neck, to end her life. She was quite hysterical when she appeared in front of the bench and was sent back to the cells until she had been seen by a doctor and was calmer. She returned a few days later and it was agreed that she wouldn't be sent to gaol, but they would endeavour to return her to her family and friends in Dymock, a small village north of Gloucester.

Death by Alcohol

A propensity to drink led to the most common reason for a prostitute to be arrested: a charge of being drunk and disorderly. This is the one universal charge common across England when identifying prostitutes in the newspaper archives. This connection between prostitution and drinking had not gone unnoticed by the authorities, particularly when it came to their deaths. Even when a prostitute had taken her own life, been murdered, or appeared to have died from causes unrelated to drink, it was still the most common cause of death. The evils of drinking were all too obvious in the swollen livers of prostitutes in post-mortems.

Elizabeth Roberts died in Liverpool in 1847, 'while in a state of intoxication' at a brothel in North Street.[21] She died quickly of 'apoplexy, produced by excessive drinking'. At this time apoplexy referred to a sudden but natural death. The reference to excessive drinking was more of a lazy presumption based on her prostitute status than an actual diagnosis, for no post mortem appears to have been carried out. This example serves to highlight the problem with prostitute deaths reported in the newspapers: they are usually there for scandalous or sensational reasons. A prostitute dying due to alcoholism fed the narrative that all prostitutes were drunks and that a horrible early death was the punishment for leading such an immoral life i.e. she brought it on herself.

Ann Baines' body was discovered 'shockingly mutilated' in 'the flint mill of Messrs. Charles Meigh and Son, at Hanley', Stoke-on-Trent.[22] There was no consideration of foul play, or negligence on the part of the mill owners, but a damning conclusion that she was so drunk that 'she became entangled in the strap of the fly-wheel' and was dragged into the system, dying instantly. It was thought she been looking for shelter from a cold spring night, which explained why she was in the mill (because sleeping outside would have seen her arrested under the Vagrancy Act). The concluding remarks of the article claimed:

> The wretched women had been several times before the magistrates for drunkenness. A few years since her husband, Charles Baines, a young man respectably connected at Hanley, poisoned himself, in a fit of desperation, bought on by excessive drinking.

It reads as if a pamphlet from the temperance movement, or a religious leader guiding his flock against the dangers of excessive drinking, not as a report on the death of a grieving woman.

The death of Mary Ann Thornton at Fish Sands, Hartlepool, in 1871 sounds equally as suspicious. She was in the company of a man named James Gallagher on the beach below a large coastal wall. It was around midnight, when three men were alerted to the fact Mary might be dead because 'she had made an extraordinary noise in her throat'.[23] They went down onto the dark sands and lit a match to allow them to see what the problem was, illuminating James 'lying upon the deceased'. He rose and said 'Polly, let us away', but she didn't respond and it was clear that she was dead. Mary was only 20.

James was arrested under suspicion of manslaughter, but the inquest stated she had died of natural causes and he was released (see page X for a newspaper article). The surgeon, Mr James Rawlings, stated her untimely death 'resulted from a number of causes, namely – that her diseased heart had been acted upon by spirits and her incorrect mode of life'. Yes, she died because she was an alcoholic prostitute. It seems remarkable that men some distance away heard her dying cries and went running, but the man she was with didn't even stop what he was doing to question if she was alive or not. He walked away a free man.

There had been a similar conclusion to the death of Martha Surfleet in Liverpool, in 1847 who was struck with a poker by her brothel keeper, Francis Downs (see page X for a newspaper article).[24] The coroner delivered a verdict of a natural death which the judge did not think correct, so another examination was requested. Again, the second surgeon agreed that she died of natural causes. The jury's final verdict was that she '"Died from excessive drinking", but added that "although the verdict was in accordance with the evidence of the surgeons, it was not, in their opinion, in accordance with justice".'[25] A sentiment that seems appropriate for all of these deaths.

Thankfully not all murders, potential, suspicious, or otherwise, went unpunished. Jane Holland was living in Crewkerne, Somerset, in 1852 when she was killed by her paramour, Charles Savage. He was jealous when she paid attention to another man when they were out drinking. A fight broke out at home later, in which he complained that she was a whore, and her mother replied 'Charles, you knowed [sic – West Country accent] that she was a w[hore] before and why did you have anything to do with her?'[26] He administered a fatal blow to Jane's head a short while later, resulting in a massive bleed to her brain. He was transported for seven years. As a refreshing aside, Jane was described as 'a woman who frequented fairs with a gingerbread stall' in the *Globe* newspaper, rather than a prostitute.[27] The paper's focus was on Charles' abominable crime, and not Jane's reputation.

There were a number of routes out of prostitution, some of which were very undesirable. The reformatories, refuges and homes were the best solutions for young girls who wished for a life other than prostitution. For those who were older and entrenched in their immoral ways, disease, destitution and death were more likely options, or so the papers would like you to think. A large number of prostitutes slipped out of their gaudy, alcohol-fuelled life and into another life of employment, marriage and motherhood. For those who married, their marriage certificate was proof of their transition from immoral to respectable, from poor to comfortable, and for a huge number of women who used prostitution as a temporary measure to survive, the knowledge of their immoral behaviour died with them. May they rest in peace.

Acknowledgements

The biggest thanks have to go to (soon to be Dr) Sophie Michell who was my virtual colleague through the whole process. Her support, guidance and friendship has kept me going, from the excitement of discovering fascinating women, to the long weeks of endless editing.

I also need to thank Dr Peter Jones for his guidance in my MRes, and encouraging me to write a book on this subject. Thanks to Alan for his persistence that I should write a book, and Jonathan for passing on a useful book and information. To my enthusiastic cheerleaders – you know who you are – I will be forever grateful for your pompom waving.

I'd also like to thank the wonderful staff at Peterborough Archives, past and present, who helped me to explore the lives of my local Victorian prostitutes, to the local history societies who have welcomed me when I have given talks on the subject, and to the ever-enthusiastic community of historians on social media.

I am indebted to the hard work and support of Amy and Karyn at Pen and Sword, who made the production and editing of the book as seamless as possible.

In addition, my thanks go to Joy, Caroline, Theresa, Charron and Russ. You are all fabulous at what you do.

Notes

Chapter 1

1. Paula Bartley, *Prostitution: Prevention and Reform in England, 1860–1914* (London: Routledge, 2000), p.5.
2. See Bibliography.
3. *Leeds Mercury*, 4 January 1840, p.7.
4. 'Savage Outrage in Hawley Croft', *Sheffield Independent*, 12 February 1868, p.3.
5. The Calendar of Prisoners contains hand-written additions of seven previous convictions.
6. *Cornubian and Redruth Times*, 3 December 1869, p.4.
7. *Luton Times and Advertiser*, 20 July 1872, p.3.
8. *North Wilts Herald*, 26 June 1875, p.5.
9. Frances Finnegan, *Poverty and Prostitution, a Study of Victorian Prostitutes in York* (Cambridge: Cambridge University Press, 1979), p.166.
10. *Lincolnshire Chronicle*, 5 October 1838, p.3.
11. *Kendal Mercury*, 13 November 1847, p.3.
12. *Westmorland Gazette*, 13 November 1847, p.3.
13. *Westmorland Gazette*, 15 January 1848, p.4.
14. He'd been blinded by a firework according to a later census.
15. South West Heritage Trust; Taunton, Somerset; Reference Number: *Q/AGS/14/2*, viewed at Ancestry.co.uk.
16. *Western Gazette*, 28 February 1868, p.5.
17. 'The Greek Church (Later St. Mary's, Crown Street) and St. Martin's Almhouses', in *Survey of London: Volumes 33 and 34, St Anne Soho*, ed. F.H.W. Sheppard (London, 1966), pp. 278–287. *British History Online* <http://www.british-history.ac.uk/survey-london/vols33-4/pp278-287> [accessed 6 February 2023]
18. *Stamford Mercury*, 6 August 1875, p.5.
19. See Chapter 6. *Northampton Mercury*, 23 March 1889, p.10.
20. *Shepton Mallet Journal*, 1 January 1869, p.2.
21. *Lincolnshire Chronicle*, 29 July 1865, p.8.
22. *Norwich Mercury*, 6 April 1859, p.6.
23. Frances Finnegan, *Poverty and Prostitution, A Study of Victorian Prostitutes in York* (Cambridge: Cambridge University Press, 1979), p.7.
24. *Maryport Advertiser*, 19 September 1891, p.5.
25. *Jarrow Express*, 4 June 1880, p.3.
26. *Birmingham Mail*, 13 November 1886, p.3.
27. It was also the word used when someone had died following a stroke.
28. *Norwich Mercury*, 12 August 1874, p.3.
29. *Norwich Mercury*, 27 October 1875, p.3.
30. Judith R. Walkowitz, *Prostitution and Victorian Society: Women, Class and the State* (Cambridge: Cambridge University Press, 1980), pp.18–9.

Chapter 2

1. 'Brewster Sessions', *Derbyshire Times*, 27 August 1859, p.3.
2. *York Herald*, 11 March 1843, p.4.
3. *Cheshire Observer*, 10 March 1883, p.6; *Illustrated Police News*, 17 March 1883, p.2.
4. 'Alleged Attempted Murder in Chester', *Illustrated Police News*, 17 March 1883, pp.1–2.
5. 'Robbery By a Prostitute', *Whitehaven News*, 10 November 1864, p.6.
6. A long wooden box seat with arms and back.
7. *Hereford Times*, 31 October 1857, p.6.
8. This also served to 'other' these women. This is the 'Voldemort' class of women – those who must not be named.
9. *Lincolnshire Chronicle*, 19 July 1838, p.2; Matilda Staff was dismissed from her charge of stealing a sovereign. She appeared in the paper after two other prostitute cases; Elizabeth Brady had been labelled an unfortunate and Maria Pinnock as a prostitute; *Norfolk News*, 13 July 1861, p.3.
10. 'Nymphs of the pavé' and 'females of the pave' were the two most 'othering' of all of the terms.
11. David Taylor, *Beerhouses, Brothels and Bobbies: Policing by Consent in Huddersfield and the Huddersfield District in the Mid-Nineteenth Century*, (Huddersfield: University of Huddersfield, 2016), p.146.
12. *Windsor and Eton Express*, 2 November 1839, p.4.
13. Gloucestershire Archives; Gloucester, Gloucestershire, England; Reference: *Q/Gc/6/4*, Ancestry.com. *Gloucestershire, England, Prison Records, 1728–1914* [database on-line]. Lehi, UT, USA: Ancestry.com Operations, Inc., 2016.
14. Ibid.
15. Peterborough, Peterborough Archives Service, PAS/PPF/2/1/1, 'Elizabeth Ashworth', City of Peterborough Police Force: Register of Previous Convictions, c.1889–1922.
16. Margot Mifflin, *Bodies of Subversion*, Revised Edition (United States, powerHouse Books, 2013) p.4; Miliann Kang and Katherine Jones, 'Why do people get tattoos?', *Contexts* 6.1 (2007): 42–47.
17. *Hereford Times*, 8 October 1859, p.6.
18. *Wolverhampton Chronicle and Staffordshire Advertiser*, 11 July 1838, p.4.
19. Ancestry.com. *Cornwall, England, Bodmin Gaol Records, 1821–1899* (database on-line). Provo, UT, USA: Ancestry.com Operations, Inc., 2016.
20. Frances Finnegan, *Poverty and Prostitution, A Study of Victorian Prostitutes in York* (Cambridge: Cambridge University Press, 1979), p.166.
21. John Woolf and Keshia N. Abraham, *Black Victorians: Hidden in History* (Richmond: Duckworth Books, 2022).

Chapter 3

1. Walter E. Houghton, *The Victorian Frame of Mind 1830–1870* (Connecticut: Yale University Press, 1957), p.366.
2. Judith R. Walkowitz and Daniel J. Walkowitz *"We are not beasts of the field": Prostitution and the poor in Plymouth and Southampton under the CDA'*, Feminist Studies, Vol 1:3/4, (1973) 73–106, <https://www.jstor.org/stable/1566481> [accessed 30 April 2023].
3. Kellow Chesney, *The Victorian Underworld* (London: Temple Smith, 1970), p.315.
4. 'The Aggravated Assault Case', *Northwich Guardian*, 17 September 1862, p.2.
5. Catherine Lee, *Policing Prostitution, 1856–1886: Deviance, Surveillance and Morality – Perspectives in Economic and Social History* (London: Routledge, 2013), p.74.
6. 'The Question of "Harbouring Prostitutes"', *Liverpool Weekly Courier*, 11 January 1868, p.4.

7. 'Publicans and Prostitutes', *Liverpool Mercury*, 10 January 1868, p.8; 'The Question of "Harbouring Prostitutes"', *Liverpool Weekly Courier*, 11 January 1868, p.4.
8. 'Publicans and Prostitutes', *Liverpool Mercury*, 10 January 1868, p.8.
9. 'Epping and Harlow Charge Against a Medical Man', *Essex Herald*, 9 April 1867, pp.7–8.
10. Chris Pond, 'The Chigwell stationmaster's wife: the notorious Debden rape case of 1867', *Loughton and District Historical Society Newsletter 193*, April-May 2012, pp.14–15, <https://loughtonhistoricalsociety.org.uk/wp-content/uploads/simple-file-list/Newsletters/Newsletter-2012/LHS-NL-193-2012-Apr-May.pdf>[accessed 30 April 2023]
11. 'Extraordinary and Most Brutal Case of Rape', *Durham Chronicle*, 24 March 1843, pp.1–3.
12. *Newcastle Journal*, 25 March 1843, p.3.
13. *Durham Chronicle*, 24 March 1843, p.3.
14. 'Bagge (Rev. J.) vs Newcomb (Rd.)', *Lincolnshire Chronicle*, 23 July 1841, p.2.
15. 'Bagge (Rev. James) vs Newcomb (Rd)', *Stamford Mercury*, 23 July 1841, p.2.
16. *Leeds Mercury*, 16 April 1857, p.3.
17. 'A Trio of Drunkards', *Worcester Journal*, 20 March 1858, p.8.
18. *Stamford Mercury*, 15 September 1865, p.5.
19. *Southern Times and Dorset County Herald*, 4 February 1882, p.6.
20. *Cambridge Independent Press*, 17 November 1855, p.7.
21. *Lincolnshire Chronicle*, 29 July 1865, p.8.
22. 'Alleged Robbery By a Prostitute', *Lincolnshire Chronicle*, 20 October 1865, p.6.
23. 'Grave Charge Disproved', *Portsmouth Evening News*, 27 June 1891, p.2.
24. 'The False Charge Against a Woman at Aldershot', *Aberdeen Free Press*, 1 July 1891, p.5.
25. *Sheffield Independent*, 1 July 1891, p.4.
26. 'The Aldershot Perjury Case Verdict', *Leicester Daily Post*, 6 August 1891, p.5.
27. *York Herald*, 7 August 1891, p.4.
28. 'Contagious Diseases Act', *Bedford Mercury*, 14 November 1874, p.5.
29. *Satirist*, 3 May 1840, p.7.
30. *Bell's New Weekly Messenger*, 14 June 1840, p.2.
31. *Stamford Mercury*, 5 June 1840, p.3.
32. *Cambridge Independent Press*, 27 June 1840, p.3.
33. *Cambridge General Advertiser*, 3 June 1840, p.2.
34. *Cambridge Chronicle and Journal*, 6 June 1840, p.2.
35. *Satirist*, 14 June 1840, p.7.
36. *Halifax Guardian*, 13 January 1844, p.5.
37. Malcolm Bull, *Malcolm Bull's Calderdale Companion*, (2023) <http://www.calderdalecompanion.co.uk/m408_b.html#b673> [accessed 30 April 2023]
38. University of York, *Yorkshire Historical Dictionary*,<https://yorkshiredictionary.york.ac.uk/words/cabin> [accessed 30 April 2023]
39. *Lincolnshire Chronicle*, 25 December 1863, p.6.
40. *Cambridge Independent Press*, 19 December 1863, p.6.
41. Ibid; *Lincolnshire Chronicle*, 25 December 1863, p.6; *Lincolnshire Chronicle*, 27 March 1863, p.6.
42. The word slop is used interchangeably with shirt and smock during the trial.
43. *Lincolnshire Chronicle*, 27 March 1863, p.6.
44. Thomas Whyle was the landlord of the George and Star and also ran the adjoining malting; Robert Gardner, *History, Gazetteer and Directory of Cambridgeshire*, (Peterborough, 1851), p.557, <https://specialcollections.le.ac.uk/digital/collection/p16445coll4/id/281872/

rec/8> [accessed 30 April 2023]; there are many references to the location of the maltings but the most useful is from the *Lincolnshire Chronicle*, 25 December 1863, p.6.

45. *Cambridge Independent Press*, 9 January 1864, p.3; *Cambridge Chronicle and Journal*, 2 January 1864, p.8.
46. *Cambridge Independent Press*, 9 January 1864, p.3.
47. Ibid.
48. *Cambridge Independent Press*, 21 March 1863, p.6.
49. *Cambridge Chronicle and Journal*, 2 January 1864, p.8.
50. *Lincolnshire Chronicle*, 25 December 1863, p.6.
51. *Cambridge Chronicle and Journal*, 2 January 1864, p.8.
52. Ibid.
53. *Lincolnshire Chronicle*, 25 December 1863, p.6.
54. *Cambridge Independent Press*, 19 December 1863, p.6.
55. *Lincolnshire Chronicle*, 25 December 1863, p.6.
56. *Cambridge Independent Press*, 19 December 1863, p.6.
57. *Lincolnshire Chronicle*, 25 December 1863, p.6.
58. *Cambridge Independent Press*, 9 January 1864, p.3.
59. Caroline Clifford, *10 Cambridgeshire Crimes* (The History Press, 2023), <https://www.thehistorypress.co.uk/articles/10-cambridgeshire-crimes/> [accessed 5 January 2023]

Chapter 4

1. *Stamford Mercury*, 14 February 1862, p.4.
2. 'The Brothel Nuisance', *West Surrey Times*, 18 April 1863, p.3.
3. The Licensing Act made it an offence for prostitutes to be found on the premises for any more than basic refreshment and the Common Lodging Houses Act of 1851 introduced legislation to ensure that rooms were single sex or for married couples and they were regularly inspected.
4. Sarah Wise, *The Blackest Streets* (London: Vintage, 2009), p.9.
5. Dean Kirby, *Angel Meadow: Victorian Britain's Most Savage Slum* (Barnsley: Pen and Sword, 2016), p.17.
6. Ibid, p.150.
7. 'Disgraceful Disclosures at Seaham Harbour', *Sunderland Daily Echo and Shipping Gazette*, 22 September 1884, p.3.
8. 'Disgusting Lgdging [*sic*] House', *Halifax Gazette*, 26 August 1854, p.5.
9. They used the word 'bed' but the word was interchangeable with mattress; *Torquay Times and South Devon Advertiser,* 8 August 1890, p.3.
10. *Torquay Times and South Devon Advertiser,* 5 August 1892, p.5.
11. 'The West Court Nuisance, Shocking Depravity', *Sheffield Independent*, 6 September 1845, p.2.
12. *Stamford Mercury*, 12 October 1883, p.4.
13. *Stamford Mercury*, 25 April 1852, p.3.
14. Catherine Lee, *Policing Prostitution, 1856–1886: Deviance, Surveillance and Morality – Perspective sin Economic and Social History* (London: Routledge, 2012), p.75.
15. Papers disagree about where he was from; *Leicester Chronicle*, 26 November 1842, p.1; *Leicester Mercury*, 19 November 1842, p.3.
16. *Nottingham Review*, 13 January 1843, p.6.
17. 'Theft of a Watch by a Prostitute', *Cumberland and Westmoreland Advertiser*, 25 October 1870, p.3.

18. According to the Vagrancy Act 1824.
19. As per the 1872 Licensing Act that could see them fined for keeping a brothel, or more commonly, for allowing them to meet there.
20. Licensing Act 1872, (35 Vic., c.94), available at <https://www.legislation.gov.uk/ukpga/Vict/35-36/94/enacted> [accessed 30 April 2023].
21. *Hertfordshire Express and General Advertiser*, 12 May 1860, p.3.

Chapter 5

1. *Stamford Mercury*, 22 December 1843, p.3.
2. *Weekly Dispatch (London)*, 16 January 1859, p.11.
3. Frances Finnegan, *Poverty and Prostitution, A Study of Victorian Prostitutes in York* (Cambridge: Cambridge University Press, 1979), p.39.
4. Frances Finnegan, *Poverty and Prostitution, A Study of Victorian Prostitutes in York* (Cambridge: Cambridge University Press, 1979), p.112.
5. *Eddowes's Shrewsbury Journal*, 28 May 1879, p.9.
6. 'Prostitutes', *Hull Advertiser*, 25 December 1846, p.6.
7. *Leicester Chronicle*, 19 August 1837, p.2.
8. *Eastern Daily Press*, 19 October 1881, p.3.
9. *Morning Herald (London)*, 21 December 1865, p.8.
10. Kellow Chesney, *The Victorian Underworld* (London: Temple Smith, 1970), p.315.
11. *Worcester Chronicle*, 13 May 1863, p.2; *Worcestershire Chronicle*, 9 November 1864, p.2.
12. *Brierly Hill, Stourbridge, Kidderminster and Dudley News*, 24 March 1877, p.8; *Croydon Advertiser and East Surrey Reporter*, 2 March 1872, p.4; *Croydon Times*, 2 June 1877, p.3.
13. Wire cards are used in the woollen industry to brush wool. Originally done by hand, this was industrialised during the eighteenth century; *Western Gazette*, 29 October 1875, p.8.
14. *Bristol Mercury*, 30 October 1875, p.6.
15. *Trowbridge Chronicle*, 15 January 1876, p.8.
16. 'Oh! Shame, Where is Thy Blush?', *Cheltenham Mercury*, 8 December 1866, p.2.
17. 'The Cheltenham "Demi-Monde"', *Cheltenham Examiner*, 12 December 1866, p.4.
18. *Cheltenham Mercury*, 22 December 1866, p.2.
19. *Bristol Times and Mirror*, 21 December 1866, p.2.
20. *Cheltenham Looker-On*, 13 February 1866, p.6.
21. R. Dighton, *Portrait of Lady Selina Henry?*, Photograph, Scottish National Portrait Gallery Print Room, National Galleries Scotland (website), (2023), <https://www.nationalgalleries.org/art-and-artists/126511/> [Accessed 30 April 2023].
22. *Newcastle Chronicle*, 5 November 1870, p.4.
23. 'Prosecution of a French Strumpet', *Stamford Mercury*, 8 March 1844, p.2.
24. Herbert married a French woman not long afterwards and shortly after that his brother George had him committed to an asylum because he was convinced he was the rightful king of England! He died in 1851 aged 43.
25. *Weekly Dispatch (London)*, 23 September 1866, p.36.
26. *Windsor and Eton Express*, 23 March 1844, p.2.
27. *Globe*, 23 May 1845, p.4.
28. *Leeds Times*, 7 June 1845, p.5.
29. *Leeds Times*, 27 December 1845, p.8.
30. *Southern Times and Dorset County Herald*, 6 November 1852, p.8.
31. *Brighton Guardian*, 21 March 1860, p.6.

32. *Brighton Guardian*, 13 June 1860, p.6.
33. *Newcastle Daily Chronicle*, 5 July 1899, p.8.
34. *Norwich Mercury*, 26 June 1861, p.3.
35. *Shields Daily News*, 3 August 1891, p.3.
36. Bucks, *Windsor and Eton Express*, 22 October 1853, p.3.)
37. *Staffordshire Advertiser*, 4 October 1845, p.3.
38. *Bolton Free Press*, 12 November 1842, p.3.
39. *Sheffield Daily Telegraph*, 18 July 1862, p.3.
40. *Beverly and East Riding Recorder*, 19 July 1862, p.4.
41. *Leeds Times*, 21 November 1846, p.5.
42. *Halifax Courier*, 17 June 1854, p.5.
43. A.W. Watkin, 'Industries of the Past Recalled', *Biggleswade Chronicle*, 28 December 1951, p.2.
44. A large loaf weighing about 4lbs or 1.8kg which could be divided up to be sold in parts.
45. The *Bedfordshire Times* believed she was 18, but the others 17.
46. *Leighton Buzzard Observer and Linslade Gazette*, 5 July 1864, p.3; *Bedford Times and Independent*, 2 July 1864, p.8; *Bucks Advertiser and Aylesbury News*, 2 July 1864, p.8; *Bedford Mercury*, 2 July 1864, p.5.
47. *Northampton Mercury*, 15 October 1864, p.7.
48. *Leighton Buzzard Observer and Linslade Gazette*, 11 October 1864, p.4.
49. *Bucks Chronicle and Bucks Gazette*, 22 October 1864, p.3.
50. *Bedfordshire Times and Independent*, 26 May 1866, p.6.
51. *Bedfordshire Times and Independent*, 1 May 1866, p.8.
52. 'Charge of Harbouring Prostitutes', *Leighton Buzzard Observer and Linslade Gazette*, 17 August 1869, p.3.
53. 'Obstructing The Police in The Execution of Their Duty', *Leighton Buzzard Observer and Linslade Gazette*, 5 July 1870, p.3.
54. Ivy Pinchbeck, *Women Workers and the Industrial Revolution, 1750–1850* (Abingdon: Frank Cass and Co., 1977), p.220.
55. 'A Ladies' Saturday Night in North End', *Leighton Buzzard Observer and Linslade Gazette*, 2 April 1872, p.3.
56. *Leighton Buzzard Observer and Linslade Gazette*, 7 August 1866, p.4.
57. 'North End Vixens', *Leighton Buzzard Observer and Linslade Gazette*, 3 June 1873, p.3.
58. *Leighton Buzzard Observer and Linslade Gazette*, 15 December 1874, p.3.
59. Pamela Horn, *The Victorian Country Child*, New Edition (Stroud: Alan Sutton Publishing, 1990), p.120.
60. Ibid, p.67.
61. Even two-year-olds could be employed in the straw plaiting Industry. Pamela Horn, *The Victorian Country Child*, New Edition (Stroud: Alan Sutton Publishing, 1990), p.124.
62. *Leighton Buzzard Observer and Linslade Gazette*, 31 October 1876, pp.2–4
63. *Luton Times and Advertiser*, 13 July 1877, p.3.
64. Juries were loathed to find women guilty of murder or manslaughter and it was quite common for them to be released even when the evidence was damning. This case hinged on the word of one witness, though, so it would be very easy for the jury to dismiss her.
65. *Bucks Herald*, 29 December 1894, p.10.
66. The queen had been a fan but knew it was no longer a viable for of income for women once machinery had been created for plaiting. *Luton Times and Advertiser*, 26 July 1895, p.3.

Chapter 6
1. Nor is it a crime in the twenty-first century in England.
2. *Cambridge Independent Press*, 24 January 1846, p.3.
3. *Staffordshire Advertiser*, 25 January 1840, p.2; *Staffordshire Gazette and County Standard*, 25 January 1840, p.3.
4. *Morning Advertiser*, 14 April 1858, p.7.
5. Jane Pearson and Maria Rayner, *Prostitution in Victorian Colchester* (Hatfield: University of Hertfordshire Press, 2018), p.114.
6. *Birkenhead News*, 3 September 1884, p.3.
7. *Portsmouth Evening News*, 12 June 1885, p.3.
8. The brothel was most likely to be in King's Lynn; *Stamford Mercury*, 26 October 1838, p.2.
9. Mary Baker, *Convict Records*, (2023), <http:/www.convictrecords.com.au/> [accessed 30 April 2023]
10. *Staffordshire Advertiser*, 24 October 1846, p.2.
11. Ibid.
12. *Wolverhampton Chronicle and Staffordshire Advertiser*, 11 July 1838, p.4.
13. *Wolverhampton Chronicle and Staffordshire Advertiser*, 17 July 1839, p.3.
14. *Cheltenham Mercury*, 9 July 1859, p.1.
15. *Manchester Courier*, 4 August 1847, p.7.
16. *Essex Standard*, 24 July 1857, p.3.
17. *Gravesend Reporter*, 26 November 1859, p.4.
18. *Derbyshire Courier*, 19 October 1861, p.3.
19. *Derbyshire Times*, 19 October 1861, p.3.
20. *Wolverhampton Chronicle*, 31 December 1845, p.4.
21. *Liverpool Mail*, 27 December 1845, p.2.
22. *Liverpool Standard and General Commercial Advertiser*, 7 April 1846, p.3.
23. *Nottingham Review*, 29 July 1842, p.2.
24. *Birmingham Mail*, 16 April 1883, p.2.
25. Each newspaper reports this event slightly differently, some saying she asked for food and one saying she gave her the breast and then took her off.
26. *Illustrated Police News*, 17 March 1883, p.2.
27. *Cheshire Observer*, 10 March 1883, p.6.
28. *Manchester Courier*, 16 April 1883, p.3.
29. *Cheshire Observer*, 10 March 1883, p.6.

Chapter 7
1. Judith R. Walkowitz, *Prostitution and Victorian Society: Women, Class and the State* (Cambridge: Cambridge University Press, 1980), p.146.
2. Vagrancy Act, 1824 (5 Geo. 4. 83), available at <https://www.legislation.gov.uk/ukpga/Geo4/5/83/section/4> [Accessed 30 April 2023].
3. The system was the same for men, but they could also face whipping in these situations, something that was not an option for women.
4. *Western Daily Mercury*, 5 January 1864, p.3.
5. *Morning Post*, 19 February 1852, p.7.
6. *Kendal Mercury*, 21 February 1852, p.6.
7. Breeches did not have a central fly like modern trousers but a wide front flap that was secured near the waistband by buttons. There were also buttons securing the waistband too.

Notes   153

8. 'Alleged Robbery', *Westmoreland Gazette*, 25 February 1871, p.6.
9. *Norfolk Chronicle*, 27 October 1855, p.2.
10. Judith R. Walkowitz's work is an excellent starting point if you are new to the subject.
11. *Bee-Hive*, 4 December 1869, p.10.
12. Treatments for syphilis, for example, were hazardous and ineffective.
13. Linda Mahood, *The Magdelenes, Prostitution in the Nineteenth Century* (London: Routledge, 1990), pp.1–2.
14. Judith R. Walkowitz, *Prostitution and Victorian Society: Women, Class and the State* (Cambridge: Cambridge University Press, 1980), p.2.
15. The term was used by the Ladies' National Association. The phrase appeared in a public letter by Mrs Hume-Rothery (a vocal member of the association) to William Gladstone which was published in some newspapers in 1870, and in an article written by Emeritus Professor F.W. Newman in the *Cheltenham Mercury*; 'The Contagious Diseases Act – The Proposed Commission of Enquiry, and an Order in Council', *Cosmopolitan*, 14 July 1870, p.12; 'The Contagious Diseases Acts', *Cheltenham Mercury*, 18 June 1870, p.2.
16. *Stamford Mercury*, 18 May 1865, p.7.
17. *Newcastle Guardian*, 2 February 1861, p.6.
18. *Hull Packet*, 7 March 1871, p.8.
19. Mrs Hume-Rothery had sadly died the year before the acts were repealed.
20. Public Health Act, (38 Vict, c.55) available at .<https://www.legislation.gov.uk/ukpga/Vict/38-39/55/contents/enacted> [accessed 30 April 2023].
21. 'The Social Evil in Luton', *Luton Times and Advertiser*, 26 February 1876, p.6.
22. *Worcestershire Chronicle*, 22 February 1879, p.6.
23. It is also hated by many for criminalising sex between men.
24. *Cornubian and Redruth Times*, 4 October 1895, p.8.
25. *Leicester Daily Post*, 3 November 1898, p.2.
26. *Post Office Directory of Cumberland 1858*, (London: Kelly and Co., 1858), p.121, <https://specialcollections.le.ac.uk/digital/collection/p16445coll4/id/80524/rec/3> [accessed 30 April 2023].
27. Ibid, p.8.
28. Ibid, p.12.
29. 'Drunk and Disorderly', *Whitehaven Post*, 15 December 1859, p.2.
30. *Cumberland Pacquet and Ware's Whitehaven Advertiser*, 31 July 1860, p.5.
31. 'Incorrigible Rogue', *Whitehaven News*, 10 July 1862, p.6.
32. *Post Office Directory of Cumberland 1858*, p.122.
33. *Whitehaven News*, 6 February 1862, p.3.
34. 'Disorderly Characters', *Cumberland Pacquet*, 19 August 1862, p.8.
35. 'Disorderly Prostitutes', *Cumberland Pacquet*, 30 September 1862, p.8.
36. *Cumberland Pacquet*, 20 January 1863, p.5.
37. 'Drunk and Disorderly', *Whitehaven News*, 6 August 1863, p.7.
38. 'Drunk and Disorderlies', *Whitehaven News*, 20 August 1863, p.2.
39. *Whitehaven News*, 21 April 1864, p.7.
40. The tone and content of the letter is a bit of an eye opener. He believes that everyone was born into a certain position and that's where they should stay; *Whitehaven News*, 28 April 1864, p.5.
41. *Barrow Herald and Furness Advertiser*, 17 December 1864, p.8.
42. *Carlisle Journal*, 14 November 1865, p.4.
43. *Cumberland Paquet and Ware's Whitehaven Advertiser*, 23 April 1863, p.8.

44. *Carlisle Examiner and North Western Advertiser*, 9 November 1867, p.3.
45. *England and Wales Criminal Registers, 1791–1892*, England, Cumberland, 1862, p.1 [Accessed via Ancestry].
46. *UK, Calendar of Prisoners, 1868–1929*, 1869, pp.444–5.
47. Ibid, 1870, p.454; The Prison Act 1865 detailed a number of offences including assaults, bad language, idleness and indecent behaviour, all of which Rosy had exhibited previously. She would have received up to three days in close confinement with bread and water, although after her assault she may have received far greater punishment; W. Cunningham Glen, *The Prison Act 1865* (London: Shaw and Sons, 1865), pp. 55–56, <https://www.google.co.uk/books/edition/The_Prison_Act_1865/fcwDAAAAQAAJ?hl=en&gbpv=1&printsec=frontcover> [accessed 30 April 2023]; *Cumberland and Westmorland Advertiser*, 5 July 1870, p.4.
48. *Jarrow Express*, 2 May 1874, p.3.
49. 'After Marriage', *Jarrow Guardian and Tyneside Reporter*, 2 January 1875, p.5.
50. 'A Sad Lass', *Jarrow Guardian and Tyneside Reporter*, 13 February 1875, p.8.
51. 'She was There Again', *Jarrow Guardian and Tyneside Reporter*, 15 October 1880, p.8.
52. *Jarrow Express*, 5 August 1881, p.3.
53. *Jarrow Express*, 16 June 1882, p.5.
54. *Jarrow Express*, 21 July 1882, p.8.
55. 'A Good Score', *Shields Daily Gazette*, 2 December 1884, p.3.

Chapter 8
1. London School of Economics and Political Science, *Charles Booth's London Poverty Maps and Police Notebooks*, (2016), <https://booth.lse.ac.uk/map/17/-0.0610/51.5127/100/0> [accessed 30 April 2023].
2. M. Chattopadhyay, S. Bandyopadhyay and C. Duttagupta, 'Biosocial Factors Influencing Women to Become Prostitutes in India', *Social Biology*, 41 (1994), pp.3–4, 252–9.
3. 'The Warning to Servant Girls', *Warrington Examiner*, 20 September 1879, p.8.
4. *Warminster Herald*, 23 November 1867, p.7.
5. 'Operation of the Contagious Diseases Act', *Eastbourne Gazette*, 21 September 1870, p.3.
6. *Birkenhead News*, 20 November 1880, p.3.
7. *Birkenhead News*, 5 July 1884, p.5.
8. 'The Social Evil in Douglas', *Isle of Man Times*, 22 August 1874, p.3; *Manchester Courier*, 15 November 1882, p.7.
9. *Hyde and Glossop Weekly News and North Cheshire Herald*, 3 February 1866, p.3.
10. *Lincolnshire Chronicle*, 27 November 1846, p.5.
11. A phrase used by the Wootton Bassett Hiring Fair; 'Wootton Bassett Hiring Fair', *Wilts and Gloucestershire Standard*, 13 October 1846, p.3.
12. *Kentish Gazette*, 10 July 1860, p.10; *Lincolnshire Chronicle*, 27 November 1846, p.5.
13. 'Hiring Fairs', *Hereford Journal*, 30 January 1861, p.3.
14. *Leicester Journal*, 4 November 1870, p.7; *Leicestershire Mercury*, 3 November 1860, p.6.
15. *Leicester Journal*, 30 October 1868, p.7.
16. *Nottinghamshire Guardian*, 9 August 1849, p.2.
17. 'A Shocking Case at Walsall', *Newcastle Guardian and Silverdale, Chesterton and Audley Chronicle*, 10 June 1893, p.6.
18. *Leicester Daily Post*, 29 July 1893, p.3.
19. *Northern Weekly Gazette*, 27 October 1877, p.6.

Chapter 9

1. Phillipa Hetherington and Julia Laite, 'Editorial Note: Special Issue: Migration, Sex and Intimate Labor', *Journal of Women's History*, Johns Hopkins University Press, Vol 33, No. 4, (2021), pp.7–39.
2. United Nations Office on Drugs and Crime, *Human Trafficking, The Crime*, <https://www.unodc.org/unodc/en/human-trafficking/crime.html> [Accessed 29 April 2023]
3. Deborah R. Brock, *Making Work, Making Trouble, The Social Regulation of Sexual Labour*, Second Edition (Toronto: University of Toronto Press, 2009), p.155.
4. *Worcester Journal*, 20 March 1858, p.8.
5. *Blackburn Standard*, 31 March 1858, p.3.
6. 'Criminal Statistics of Blackburn', *Preston Chronicle*, 29 October 1859, p.6.
7. *Morning Herald (London)*, 26 March 1863, p.8.
8. There is still information flittering around the internet about her supposed spontaneous combustion. It was nothing of the sort. He first hit Miss Pulley in the face before strangling her to death. He later returned to set her body alight to destroy the evidence of his murder.
9. *Lincolnshire Chronicle*, 16 April 1858, p.1.
10. *Stamford Mercury*, 4 May 1860, p.4.
11. Ibid.
12. *Leamington Spa Courier*, 30 May 1846, p.4.
13. 'Traffic in Prostitution', *Reynold's Newspaper*, 25 June 1854, p.6.
14. *Liverpool Mail*, 9 September 1854, p.3.
15. 'Procuration of Prostitution by Fraud and Intimidation', *Hull Packet*, 27 October 1854, pp.7–8.
16. 'Abduction of Young Girls', *London Evening Standard*, 7 September 1854, p.3.
17. 'The Abduction of English Girls by Foreign Prostitutes', *London Weekly Investigator*, 27 March 1856, p.2.
18. 'Importation of Young German Girls into England', *Sheffield Daily Telegraph*, 17 September 1864, p.6.
19. *Leeds Times*, 27 February 1858, p.8.
20. *Morning Advertiser*, 24 June 1856, p.7.
21. *Worcestershire Chronicle*, 2 December 1857, p.4.
22. 'Export of English Girls for Prostitution', *Western Times*, 22 March 1862, p.10.
23. The full series of articles in the Pall Mall newspaper were published in a book by Stead and is available for free online; *Pall Mall Gazette* Secret Commission, Maiden Tribute of Modern Babylon, (1885), <https://www.google.co.uk/books/edition/Maiden_Tribute_of_Modern_Babylon/cktFAQAAMAAJ?hl=en&gbpv=1&printsec=frontcover> [accessed 30 April 2023].
24. *Morning Post*, 1 October 1885, p.5.
25. *Stamford Mercury*, 17 May 1850, p.2.
26. *Stamford Mercury*, 10 April 1863, p.5.
27. *Reynold's Newspaper*, 29 November 1885, p.3.
28. *Kentish Gazette*, 21 July 1874, p.5.
29. Trial of Sir Capel Fitzgerald, The Proceedings of the Old Bailey Online, <www.oldbaileyonline.org>, version 8.0 [accessed 30 April 2023].
30. *Illustrated Police News*, 20 July 1878, p.2.
31. 'Assault on "The Great Vance"', *The Era*, 12 December 1885, p.10.
32. 'The Great Vance', *The Era*, 10 April 1886, p.10.

Chapter 10
1. *Yorkshire Gazette*, 14 August 1841, p.3.
2. *North and South Shields Gazette and Northumberland and Durham Advertiser*, 24 May 1850, p.5.
3. This was his cause of death stated on his death certificate.
4. Peter Higginbotham, 'St Matthew's Industrial Home for Girls, Ipswich, Suffolk', *Children's Homes* (2023) <http://www.childrenshomes.org.uk/IpswichIH/> [accessed 30 April 2023].
5. *Framlingham Weekly News*, 14 October 1871, p.4.
6. *Portsmouth Times and Naval Gazette*, 18 June 1870, p.8.
7. *Nuneaton Observer*, 6 January 1893, p.5.
8. *Shields Daily Gazette*, 3 December 1880, p.2.
9. 'Oxford Home for Friendless Girls', *Oxford Chronicle and Reading Gazette*, 30 November 1889, p.2.)
10. 'Oxford: Board of Guardians', *Oxfordshire Weekly News*, 9 December 1891, p.7.)
11. Ibid.
12. *Shields Daily Gazette*, 6 January 1886, p.3.
13. *Birmingham Daily Post*, 12 January 1864, p.2; *Liverpool Weekly Courier*, 16 March 1878, p.4.
14. *Beverley and East Riding Recorder*, 22 February 1873, p.3.
15. *Exeter and Plymouth Gazette Daily Telegrams*, 29 February 1876, p.2.
16. Lynn Hollen Lees, *The Solidarities of Strangers* (Cambridge: Cambridge University Press, 1998), pp. 150–151.
17. *Shepton Mallet Journal*, 22 March 1867, p.3.
18. 'Determined Suicide of a Boston Prostitute', *Boston Guardian*, 31 March 1877, p.2.
19. *Morpeth Herald*, 25 May 1889, p.6.
20. *Gloucester Journal*, 20 May 1848, p.3.
21. *Liverpool Mail*, 16 October 1847, p.3.
22. *Sheffield Daily News*, 20 March 1858, p.3.
23. *York Herald*, 15 July 1871, p.9.
24. *Liverpool Standard and General Commercial Advertiser*, 6 April 1847, p.6.
25. *Liverpool Mercury*, 9 April 1847, p.8.
26. *Southern Times and Dorset County Herald*, 6 November 1852, p.8.
27. *Globe*, 2 April 1853, p.4.

Bibliography and Suggested Reading

Acton, William, *Prostitution Considered in its Moral, Social and Sanitary Aspects* (London: John Churchill, 1857)

Arnold, Catherine, *City of Sin: London and Its Vices* (London: Simon and Schuster, 2011)

Attwood, Nina, *The Prostitute's Body: Rewriting Prostitution in Victorian Britain* (London: Routledge, 2011)

Barret-Ducrocq, Françoise, *Love in the Time of Victoria* (London: Verso, 1991)

Bartley, Paula, *Prostitution: Prevention and Reform in England, 1860–1914* (London: Routledge, 2000)

Best, Geoffrey, *The History of British Society: Mid-Victorian Britain 1851–1875* (London: Weidenfeld and Nicholson, 1971)

Brock, Deborah R., *Making Work, Making Trouble: The Social Regulation of Sexual Labour*, Second Edition (Toronto: University of Toronto Press, 2009)

Chesney, Kellow, *The Victorian Underworld* (London: Temple Smith, 1970)

Collini, Stefan, *Public Moralists, Political Thought and Intellectual Life in Britain 1850–1930* (Oxford: Clarendon Press, 1991)

Crick, Emma, *An Untold Story: Experiences of Life and Street Prostitution in Hull* (Hull Lighthouse Project, 2017)

Della Giusta, Marina, Maria Laura Di Tomasso and Steinar Strøm, *Sex markets, A denied Industry* (London: Routledge, 2008)

Engels, Friedrich, *The Condition of the Working Class in England* (Oxford: Oxford University Press, 2009)

Finnegan Frances, *Poverty and Prostitution, A Study of Victorian Prostitutes in York* (Cambridge: Cambridge University Press, 1979)

Fisher, Trevor, *Prostitution and the Victorians* (Stroud: Sutton Publishing, 1997)

Garton, Stephen, *Histories of Sexuality, Antiquity to Sexual Revolution* (London: Routledge, 2004)

Gerzina, Gretchen H. (ed)., *Britain's Black Past* (Liverpool: Liverpool University Press, 2020)

Glen, W. Cunningham, *The Prison Act 1865* (London: Shaw and Sons, 1865)

Gurnham, Richard, *The Nymphs of the Pavement: Sin, Scandals and Vice in Victorian Lincolnshire* (Stroud: The History Press, 2014)

Henderson, Tony, *Disorderly Women in Eighteenth-Century London, Prostitution and Control in the Metropolis 1730–1830* (London: Routledge, 2016)

Houghton, Walter, E., *The Victorian Frame of Mind 1830–1870* (Connecticut: Yale University Press, 1957)

Hufton, Olwen, *The Prospect Before Her: A History of Women in Western Europe, 1500–1800* (New York: Vintage, 1998)

Jackson, Lee, *Palaces of Pleasure: From Music Halls to the Seaside to Football, How the Victorians Invented Mass Entertainment* (New Haven and London: Yale University Press, 2019)

Kara, Siddharth, *Sex Trafficking: Inside the Business of Modern Slavery* (New York: Columbia University Press, 2010)

Karras, Ruth Mazo, *Common Women: Prostitution and Sexuality in Medieval England* (Oxford: Oxford University Press, 1996)

Kirby, Dean, *Angel Meadow: Victorian Britain's Most Savage Slum* (Barnsley: Pen and Sword, 2016)

Lee, Catherine, *Policing Prostitution, 1856–1886: Deviance, Surveillance and Morality – Perspective sin Economic and Social History* (London: Routledge, 2013)

Lister, Kate, *A Curious History of Sex* (London: Unbound, 2020)

Lister, Kate, *Harlots, Whores and Hackabouts: A History of Sex for Sale* (London: Thames and Hudson, 2021)

London Feminist History Group, *The Sexual Dynamics of History* (London: Pluto Press, 1983)

Mahood, Linda, *The Magdelenes: Prostitution in the Nineteenth Century* (London: Routledge, 1990)

Mason, Michael, *The Making of Victorian Sexual Attitudes* (Oxford: Oxford University Press, 1994)

Mayhew, Henry and Others, *The London Underworld in the Victorian Period: Authentic First-Person Accounts by Beggars, Thieves and Prostitutes* (USA: Dover Publications Inc., 2015)

Mifflin, Margot, *Bodies of Subversion*, Revised Edition (United States: powerHouse Books, 2013)

Murdoch, Lydia, *Daily Life of Victorian Women* (Westport: Greenwood, 2014)

Pearsall, Ronald, *The Worm in the Bud: The World of Victorian Sexuality* (Stroud: Sutton, 2003)

Pearson, Jane and Maria Rayner, *Prostitution in Victorian Colchester* (Hatfield: University of Hertfordshire Press, 2018)

Riddell, Fern, *The Victorian Guide to Sex: Desire and Deviance in the 19th Century* (Barnsley: Pen and Sword, 2014)

Rubenhold, Hallie, *The Five: The Untold Lives of the Women Killed by Jack the Ripper* (London: Transworld, 2019)

Steinbach, Susie, *Women in England 1760–1914: A Social History* (London: Phoenix, 2005)

Taylor, David, *Beerhouses, Brothels and Bobbies: Policing by Consent in Huddersfield and the Huddersfield District in the Mid-Nineteenth Century* (Huddersfield: University of Huddersfield Press, 2016)

Walkowitz, Judith R., *Prostitution and Victorian Society: Women, Class and the State*, (Cambridge: Cambridge University Press, 1980), p.146.

Williams, Lucy, *Wayward Women: Female Offending in Victorian England* (Barnsley: Pen and Sword, 2016)

Williams, Lucy and Barry Godfrey, *Criminal Women 1850–1920: Researching the Lives of Britain's Female Offenders* (Barnsley: Pen and Sword, 2018)

Wise, Sarah, *The Blackest Streets* (London: Vintage, 2009)

Woolf, John and Keshia N. Abraham, *Black Victorians: Hidden in History* (Richmond: Duckworth Books, 2022), Kindle edition.

Useful Websites

https://www.ancestry.co.uk/ Ancestry UK – large database of family history records

http://www.booth.lse.ac.uk/map/ Charles Booth's Poverty Maps and Police Notebooks

https://www.britishnewspaperarchive.co.uk/ The British Newspaper Archive – large database of newspapers dating back to the eighteenth century

http://www.childrenshomes.org.uk/ Children's Homes by Peter Higginbotham

https://www.findmypast.co.uk/ Findmypast – large database of family history records including the 1921 census https://www.freereg.org.uk/ FreeReg – Free parish record database of Birth, Marriage and Burial records

https://www.greatyarmouthpreservationtrust.org/the-rows Great Yarmouth Preservation Trust project on the Rows

https://www.gro.gov.uk/gro/content/ General Register Office – the best location to buy Birth Marriage and Death (BMD) records

https://maps.nls.uk/ National Libraries of Scotland Map Images from across Britain and beyond

https://www.oldbaileyonline.org/ The Proceedings of the Old Bailey, London's Central Criminal Court, 1674 to 1913, a great site for London legal cases.

https://www.oldmapsonline.org/ Old Maps Online Zoomable historical maps from around the world

http://www.workhouses.org.uk/ Workhouses by Peter Higginbotham

Index

Dear Reader,

We hope you have enjoyed this book, but why not share your views on social media? You can also follow our pages to see more about our other products: facebook.com/penandswordbooks or follow us on Twitter @penswordbooks

You can also view our products at www.pen-and-sword.co.uk (UK and ROW) or www.penandswordbooks.com (North America).

To keep up to date with our latest releases and online catalogues, please sign up to our newsletter at: www.pen-and-sword.co.uk/newsletter

If you would like a printed catalogue with our latest books, then please email: enquiries@pen-and-sword.co.uk or telephone: 01226 734555 (UK and ROW) or email: uspen-and-sword@casematepublishers.com or telephone: (610) 853-9131 (North America).

We respect your privacy and we will only use personal information to send you information about our products.

Thank you!